So Happy and Grateful

Antonio T.Smith, Jr

So Happy and Grateful
The Universal Laws of Happiness and You

Wild Dreams Publishing
A publication of Wild Dreams Publishing
Traralgon, Vic
© 2018 by Wild Dreams Publishing

So Happy And Grateful: The Universal Laws of Happiness

And You / Antonio T. Smith, Jr.

So Happy and Grateful

Antonio T.Smith, Jr

Contents

So Happy and Grateful

                 Antonio T.Smith, Jr

So Happy and Grateful

Antonio T.Smith, Jr

So Happy and Grateful

Antonio T.Smith, Jr

One Last Thing

BELIEVE

CHAPTER 13

About The Author

So Happy and Grateful

Antonio T.Smith, Jr

Connect With Me

Join our online community to stay inspired, network, and to find other *HAPPY PEOPLE.* Visit https://www.facebook.com/groups/peoplewhoplant better/

This book comes with tons of resources for you to stay happy, get happy, and share happiness. Visit https://www.sohappyseries.com to access all the resources you need to live out the highest expression of yourself.

So Happy and Grateful

Antonio T.Smith, Jr

Follow Me Online:

Instagram:

http://instagram.com/theatsjr

Facebook:

http://facebook.com/theatsjr

Snapchat:

https://www.snapchat.com/add/theatsj

r

Twitter:

http://twitter.com/theatsjr

Podcast   Apple |

http://apple.co/2pAUvvZ

YouTube | http://bit.ly/SubPlzATS

So Happy and Grateful

Antonio T.Smith, Jr

Speaker Hub |
https://speakerhub.com/speaker/anton
io-t-smith-jr

So Happy and Grateful

Antonio T.Smith, Jr

Dedication

This book is dedicated to Serena Brown Travis, the youngest daughter of the great Les Brown. Serena, you are my friend, we have been through some tough times together— all worth it. We have built some major companies together — all profitable. Yet, neither of these reasons are why I chose to dedicate this book to you. In fact, my reasoning is very simple. You embody all the principles in this book. I have

So Happy and Grateful

Antonio T.Smith, Jr

watched you maintain your high level of happiness, no matter what information has come your way. You are brilliant and your loving family is a protective shield of happiness that encapsulates your own happiness. In truth, I could not have dedicated this book to anyone else but you. Our friendship has been an experience for the ages. I've watched you grow as a speaker and your first sermon was absolutely amazing. When it comes to speaking, you are a chip off the old block, that is for sure. You have your dad's gift to communicate — and that is one heck of a gift. If

So Happy and Grateful

Antonio T.Smith, Jr

you drank beer, I would say that I owe you one, but since you don' t, I will just dedicated a book for you. That seems like a pretty fair trade off to me. Thank you for all you have ever done for me, and thank you for changing the world. See you soon. Tell your husband I will give your beer to him.

Best,

Antonio T. Smith, Jr.

Foreword By:

Les Brown

So Happy and Grateful is one of the most poignant and encouraging pieces of work that I've read in a very longtime. It is hard to understand that happiness is a choice, even in the most adverse circumstances but this book will shift your thinking, upset and erase any former thoughts of life's misfortune.

So Happy and Grateful

Antonio T.Smith, Jr

Antonio, such as myself had a tough life···really tough. We share the same feelings of abandonment, betrayal, and loneliness during our tender years; years when we should have enjoyed every aspect of our lives, we faced hunger, sleepless nights, and worry.

"You are a winner, even if you haven't learned how to win!" - Antonio T. Smith Jr., embodies one of my favorite reminders and original quotes to "Believe in someone else's belief in you until your own belief kicks in."

Oftentimes we focus on things that are wrong, our failures, or where we are weak, I believe we are to make our valley lows become our life's peak experiences. So whether you need to as Antonio suggests, change your atmosphere, or get new relationships, know that there is no such thing as bad news···not ever and you can NEVER be defeated. My favorite book says, In ALL things give thanks. Trust me, this is one major key to happiness.

The truth is, no matter what, we have every reason to be SO HAPPY AND GRATEFUL! I am so happy and grateful for my struggles, because it made me stronger. I am so happy and grateful for my setbacks, because it only set me up for a stronger comeback. I am so happy and grateful for my life, the good and the bad, the ups and downs; it has only made me who I am.

I don't know what you are up against and I don't know what you are facing. But here's what I know about you without even knowing you. You've got something special, you've got greatness in you, and I know it's possible that you can live your dream.

If you fell down yesterday, remember to be So Happy and Grateful that you can stand up today! Go and find the winner within.

There's greatness in you!

P.S. I am so proud of Antonio. He has become one of my business advisor, coaches, and spiritual sons. He is like a brother to my children and I am so grateful that our paths have crossed.

–Les

So Happy and Grateful

Antonio T.Smith, Jr

Happiness

PART I

Chapter 1 & Intro

Geniuses Are Fools

For hundreds and maybe even thousands of years, people have studied depression and psychological illnesses. Both of these subjects are something I have studied for decades, but I have also studied the field of happiness. During the 1980s, anyone telling you they actively studied happiness was laughed at. Rightfully so, I suppose. People have been taught to fear happiness. Happiness is for rich people, and rich people are evil people. Therefore, if you want to be normal, don't be happy, be serious — you fool. Well, I encourage you all to be fools, because it is the idiots of this world that change communities and even the world. Every genius that has ever walked this earth, every

So Happy and Grateful

Antonio T.Smith, Jr

single thought leader that dared to lead his or her field in detailed knowledge have all been called "fools." In fact, the world is very unkind to geniuses until they die. Once a genius dies, then the masses appreciate him or her and wishes his or her presence was still in physical form. History is not kind to its leaders until its leaders *are* history. Let that sink in for a moment. During the 1990s, the happiness field of study would gain credibility and now, in the 21st century, people like me study happiness and teach it all over the world. There is even an official name for this field; it is called Positive Psychology.

Happiness Leads To Everything

Before we go any further, you should understand first and foremost, that happiness is guaranteed to help you achieve your other goals, have better relationships, and do better on your jobs— because people will actually like you. Go figure. Whatever you are pursuing in life, happiness will help you get there further and faster. Sure, there are angrier ways to get to your goals, but for some of you, you achieve a form of happiness when you are upset, so it is that angry-happiness that got you to where you wanted to be. However, many people like me will argue that getting somewhere without happiness is to limit where you could have arrived. Happiness is stronger than any of us will ever understand.

Happiness Is More Complex Than You Think

There is a very peculiar thing that occurs when you study happiness. As you collect data and follow people for years, (this kind of research has been conducted since the 1980s, and beyond, as for me, I have been collecting data on people's happiness since I was about 10. Weird? I know, but I didn't grow up like a normal child. I didn't play with toys after I was six and I only ever watched two cartoons in my life — maybe three,) you discover that more things and more money don't translate into more happiness. Money makes you happy. Don't let anyone tell you differently. The money will make you happy, exceedingly happy, but to a certain point. Let me explain. If you are homeless, living under a bridge in cold weather, with chapped lips, eating rotten food out of a trash can, while keeping yourself warm by insulating your clothes with old newspapers, and someone were to give you $10,000, your happiness level would skyrocket! Think about this for a moment. A mere $10,000 would make you feel equally as happy as receiving $1,000,000 in this scenario because your basic needs were met and then exceeding, and your security level changed drastically. Let's return to

So Happy and Grateful

Antonio T.Smith, Jr

the homeless and receiving $10,000 scenario. If in three more days, you were to receive another $20,000, you would be $20,000 happier. However, if you were a millionaire, earning $10,000 would not have the same effect on you than the homeless person. In other words, the millionaire would not become $10,000 happier. If you were a billionaire, I could imagine sneaking $10,000 into your bank account, and you wouldn' t even notice it. Now, here is where it gets tricky. Once you meet all your basic needs and then put yourself into the overflow, your happiness expectations will change. Security will no longer drive you, but acceptance. You will now want someone to share your safety with, or friends to share your happy moments with you. Of course, this scenario considers information that was first introduced to the world by Maslow's Hierarchy of Needs, in a paper Abraham Maslow wrote in 1943 proposing his theory.

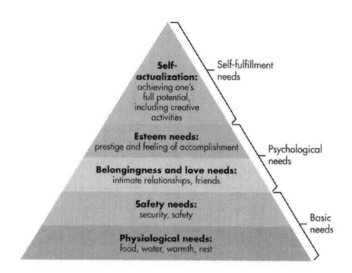

Happiness seems to get even more complex than being homeless. Psychologist Sonja Lyubomirsky discusses the "happiness set point," in her book, *The How of Happiness.* She suggests that 50 percent of happiness is genetically predetermined, while 10% is due to life circumstances, and 40 percent is the result of your outlook. Here is what's crazier than that. She is citing strong evidence and research about this "happiness set point," which comes from a series of studies that followed identical and fraternal twins. Many people have since cited this research, and this is now called the "50-10-40% formula". Below is a picture of how this looks.

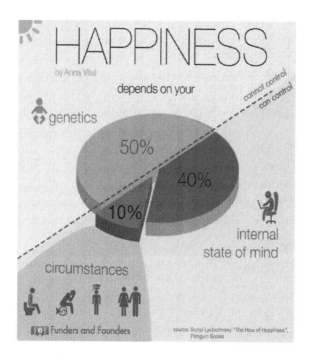

Of course, some people disagree with this. I don't blame them, nor do I blame you should you disagree. However, I have a vast understanding of genetics and neurology, and Cognitive Behavioral Therapy. In truth, these three fields of study don't completely solve all the problems against this research, but I will introduce what might be a new concept for you, but is backed by hard science— *personality begins before birth*. Here is an excerpt from an article in Psychology Today.

[1]

---

[1]
https://www.psychologyt oday.com/blog/the-favorit e-child/201010/personalit y-begins-birth

" Research indicates that even before birth, mothers' moods may affect child development, " comments Dr. Catherine Monk, a researcher at Columbia University. In summarizing Monk's work, Anne Murphy Paul in her recent cover story for Time magazine writes, "that a pregnant woman's mental state can shape her offspring's psyche. " These observations and those of others investigating fetal origins, the study of how the nine months

So Happy and Grateful

Antonio T.Smith, Jr

of gestation influences physical, mental, intellectual, and emotional functioning, mirror empirical observations long noted by mental health providers.

Ladies and gentlemen, this is scary. Why? Because were are not nice to each other as human beings, and many people are in a relationship with one another while hating each other. It is very common these days to love someone's body parts and confuse that love with actual love. Or to love not being alone, and to confuse this feeling of security with real love. As a result, we argue back and forth with our significant others, and we begin to shape our children' s personalities.

On the other hand, let' s say you don ' t argue back and forth. Your environment can affect your mood, and this will shape your child ' s personality if you are the mother. Think of it this way. If your country goes to war and your homeland becomes a war zone, and food becomes scarce, your mood will tell your unborn child that you love him or her very much, but the world is a terrifying place. Consequently, your child will be more prone to having a personality that displaces fear, and a body that has a slower metabolism, because the child has been taught from the womb that food is scarce, so the body slows down the metabolism of the child to increase chances of survival. Although this seems like a hypothetical situation, this happened with many children born during the Great Depression of America. We, as parents and future parents, have a responsibility to master our happiness to pass that part of our DNA down to our children. Something to think about as we move forward.

This Is Not A Religious Book

To be clear, I am going to argue throughout this entire book that you can transcend genetic and cultural limitations that have been put on you to decide your current level of happiness. Your happiness-meter should be as large as airports, not the hangers, but the entire airports. In fact, if you can think of something larger, which you know you can, make your happiness-meter that big because that is what you deserve. Those things that people tell you to focus on won't necessarily make you happier, but your intended behavior always will.

You deserve to be happy, and there is a universal way to achieve your happiness. In truth, you were happy when you were a baby, and we made you sour, or neutral, or whatever. I have full confidence that this book will change your outlook on happiness.

If you are religious, this book may help you find peace as you grow in awareness. If you are not religious, this book will help you find peace as you grow in knowledge. This book contains no religious bias. It has been written for all people of all planets. Planets? I just wanted to see if you were reading. Although, life on other " planets " seems scientifically possible, as we understand science today.

This book does not reject anyone's religion but adds to it. You are not meant to replace your religion with these laws if you are religious, but understand that your religion has

So Happy and Grateful

Antonio T.Smith, Jr

already encompassed these laws. You may have just missed them.

The Book Is Fighting A Few Things

First, this book is designed to fight against your dogmatic beliefs, generally given to you by religious establishments, but this is not always the case. Whatever the case, you have some beliefs within you that have stopped you from living to your ultimate level of happiness. This book will focus only on the universal Law of Happiness. The laws steep into science and logic, and what is universally understood as natural law. Like a baby sucks on a mothers milk, there is no need to understand religion to live in happiness. It will be up to you to increase your awareness to know that when his or her mother feeds an infant, that infant becomes instantly happy without the aide of religion, finances, employment, or many of the things that we say makes one happy. There is something universal in play when a baby smiles. We will only discuss what is universal.

So Happy and Grateful

Antonio T.Smith, Jr

Next, we will combat the hedonic treadmill, also known as hedonic adaptation. The hedonic treadmill is the tendency for humans to go back to being what is a "reasonable" level of happiness for them after something of significant positivity or negativity changes their circumstances or environment. [2] According to this theory, as a

---

[2] The Hedonic Treadmill states that regardless of what happens to someone, their level of happiness will return to their baseline after the event. What does this mean? It means that if you get married, move into a new house, get a promotion, loose a job or suffer an accident, for example, after a certain period of time you're likely to return to your set point.

person makes more money, expectations, and desires

rise in tandem, which results in no permanent gain in

happiness.[3]

There is the initial spike in happiness, or sadness; however, as time goes on, the feeling of happiness or sadness caused by an event starts to dissipate, habituation kicks in···. After some time has passed, you are back at the level of happiness that you were at before. (See graphic to the right for a visual)

https://positivepsycholog yprogram.com/hedonic-trea dmill/

[3] Brickman and Campbell first described the Hedonic Treadmill in 1971 stating that processes similar to sensory adaptation occur when people emotionally respond to different life events.

They suggested that our emotional system goes back to the level prior to the event, after some time. This finding was extremely significant and became central for scientists studying happiness.

One of the most notable examples of the hedonic treadmill is a study that examined people who won the lottery for a large amount of money and victims in accidents that resulted in paralysis including quadriplegic and paraplegic victims. In 1987, Brickman, Coates, & Janoff-Bulman published the study: "Lottery winners and accident victims: is happiness relative?"

https://positivepsycholog yprogram.com/hedonic-trea dmill/

So Happy and Grateful

Antonio T.Smith, Jr

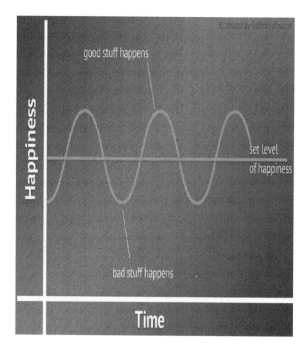

Lastly, this book is written to fight any sadness you may have in your life right now. I do not mean to imply that you should never become sad, but people who have true happiness bounce back from adversity faster than those who do not. I want to give you *bounce back power*. I want to teach you how to obtain true happiness so you can spread that happiness forward into this world.

I only ask you of one thing: pass what you have learned into from this book to someone who needs it when you are done. Please. There are far too many people who are sad, or suffer from low self-esteem. Give this book away! Remember the laws, and share them. If you are a motivational speaker or a podcaster, or any person of influence, share these rules with your communities. Don't hold on to this knowledge. Remember, with happiness, the more you have, the more everyone has!

So Happy and Grateful

Antonio T.Smith, Jr

Transformational Exercises

1. Identify limiting behaviors and limiting thinking

- Take a piece of paper and draw a line in the middle to split the paper in half. This could be a vertical or horizontal line. On one side of the paper write **Loved It**. On the other side of the paper write **Loathed It**. This is what I

So Happy and Grateful

Antonio T.Smith, Jr

call the *Loved It–Loathed It* list.
For the next 7 days, write
everything that you do. From the
moment you wake up to the moment
you go to bed. Write down every
task, including picking up the
kids to cooking dinner. If you
love or loved doing the task, put
it on the *Loved It* side of your
list. If you loathe (hate) or
loathed doing the task, put it on
the *Loathed It* side of your list.
If the take is neutral to you, put
it on the *Loathed It* side of your
list as well. Do not put anything

on your *Loved It* side of your list unless you truly love it. If you repeat task daily, you only need to write it down once. After 7 days, look at your list and see which side has more task written on it, most people will see that their *Loathed It* list is 85% longer than the loved it list. If your list is more negative than positive, make a mental note that you cannot be successful without being happy. There is no need to panic if your list has more negatives and positives. Simply replace tasks with what you love and assign someone else to do the task you hate or do something you love while doing the things that you have. For instance, if you hate cleaning but love reading, listen to an audiobook while cleaning your living space.

2. List the ways your religion has limited your thinking, concerning happiness and abundance. After your list is complete, research your sacred texts or ask a qualified spiritual leader in your religion on how to find

harmony with the abundance and happiness.

- If you want to talk to me directly about the possibility of misinterpreting your sacred texts, concerning abundance and happiness, join my Facebook group called "People Who Plant Better " at fb.com/groups/peoplewhoplantbe tter

So Happy and Grateful

Antonio T.Smith, Jr

Instructions To Have Bounce Back Power

1. Be transparent

   - There are no things that can change your life if you keep denying their existence. You must have a healthy level of self-awareness to truly be happy.

2. Stay in the plane

   - Happiness is not a jet flight to your dreams. It is a long, across the world flight. Get ready for a very long flight and stay on the plane. If you jump out the plan, you will be torn apart by the turbulence outside.

3. Change your perception

  – There is no such thing as bad news, there is only the way you perceive the information coming at you. If you change your perception, your happiness level will increase dramatically and almost overnight.

4. Change your atmosphere

- Sometimes a change in your environment will allow you to change your mood. If you can change your mood, you can change the level of your happiness.

5. Fill yourself with positivity

- You cannot be an empty cup that pours into people, even strong people get tired of being strong. Read books, listen to motivational videos on YouTube, talk to the right people or anything that serves your happiness.

6. A breakdown is not the end of the world

   – Having a bad moment is not the same as having a bad day. There is no need to drag a moment out to make it a bad day. This is not the end of the world. Relax.

7. Forgive yourself when you fail

   – You are not perfect. Be happy with who you are and improve yourself for you— not for other people.

Defining Your Happiness

THE LAW OF INTEGRITY

Chapter 2

What Is Your Definition of Happiness

So Happy and Grateful

Antonio T.Smith, Jr

Life is good. Every day of your life has been good, and this is true. There is not much of an argument for this; however, about 97% of the people on this earth will disagree vehemently with this. Nevertheless, I will be right. *Life is good. Every day of your life has been good.*

Since the beginning of time, humans have been trying to understand happiness. Aristotle[1] once wrote, "The

---

[1] Ancient Greek philosopher Aristotle was born circa 384 B.C. in Stagira, Greece. When he turned 17, he enrolled in Plato's Academy. In 338, he began tutoring Alexander the Great.

primary concern of philosophy should be, how should we live to be happy?" This is a great question and one you have asked yourself and put into action whether you are aware of it or not. Simply stated, every decision you have ever made has been a step towards what makes you happy or a get away from people and circumstances that are keeping you from happiness.

To move you forward and allow you to have your greatest life, we need to define what happiness is to you. This is very important because when it comes to happiness, you need to start with

---

https://www.biography.com
/people/aristotle-9188415

So Happy and Grateful

Antonio T.Smith, Jr

the end in mind. You are unique; therefore, you have a particular set of needs and desires that are unique to you. Happiness is subjective, meaning it can differ from person to person, but the way to obtain happiness is objective, meaning it is universal and without change. In truth, what will make me happy won't necessarily make you happy. For instance, in this part of my life, it is a huge deal for me to be one of the most respected authors in my generation, not for vanity, but I have an ultimate end goal that depends on it. As a result, releasing multiple

So Happy and Grateful

Antonio T.Smith, Jr

books a year, in different categories, and to have people love them and buy them will make me very happy. However, you may not be an author and sitting at a desk, or a perfectly lit Starbucks writing a book may be torture for you. In fact, I know people who hate writing just as much as they hate math. So, writing would be nowhere in there happiness equation unless they were writing a million dollar check to themselves. Then, they would be super happy— maybe even you.

No one can ever dictate happiness to another person. Unfortunately, this happens every day when parents tell their children what car to buy and what person to date, or when friends give each other bad financial advice, and many different scenarios. Here is a tip that will help you in life, *"although something matters to you, that does not mean that it matters to whoever you are trying to defend or help."* Many friendships have been ruined because people tried to tell others how they should be happy and what happiness looks like for them. Happiness is a purely subjective and personal decision.

So Happy and Grateful

Antonio T.Smith, Jr

Your happiness has always been your primary responsibility in life. At some point in life, we all forget to put us first. If you needed a nudge back in the right direction, here you go. You are amazing, and you deserve to be happy. Let' s define it for you.

Defining Your Happiness

A standard exercise in seminars is for you to write down on a piece of paper, "I will be happy if. " Once you have written this down, come up with definite and very detailed reasons of what would make you happy right now. Be very specific and do not mince words. You are building your future life, and you deserve to have a wonderful life. How you build it now is how you will live it later. Build with great expectancy. Make sure you complete this sentence with as many answers as possible. If you do this, it will be far easier for you to enjoy your life more than the average person.

The craziest thing about happiness is that everyone wants it, but very few have written down and defined what it means to them. Ask yourself an honest question. Have you written down what makes you happy in detail and developed a definite plan to obtain it? If not, then you are part of the 97% of people who trade their time for money, and there is about a 98% chance that you are not 100% happy with your life. Allow me to be direct with you for a moment. If you are not 100% satisfied, *you or some person or thing(s) are robbing you of life that you deserve— 99% happiness is NOT worthy of you.* Capiche?[2] All human

---

[2] Capiche is the standard English spelling of the word, usually followed by a question mark, meaning do you understand? It comes from the Italian capisci.

So Happy and Grateful

Antonio T.Smith, Jr

movement is because of dissatisfaction. If you were perfectly happy, you would never do anything with your life, ever. On the other end of the spectrum, if you are unhappy with your life right now, or completely dissatisfied, you are also the most motivated person on planet earth, should you choose to change your perception and write down your happiness.

There is another way to define happiness for you; I use it in my seminars. Imagine yourself dead, and

The word occasionally appears in several other spellings, including capeesh and capische, but these are far less common than the standard one.
http://grammarist.com/spe
lling/capiche/

So Happy and Grateful

Antonio T.Smith, Jr

the people you love the most are giving expressions at your funeral. Take what each person has said and then condense their short talk into one to two words. Do this for all the people who you love the most, not the ones who love you the most. Instead, focus on those you love and respect the most because their opinions matter to you the most. When you are finished, you will have one to two words for each one. When you figure out what each of these words are, you will discover exactly what happiness is to you. These words will become your blueprint for life. Let me show you. Here are mine:

Leader

    Driven

    Good Listener

    Genuine

    Provider

As you can see, the word "leader" is number one for me. This means that anything I do in life that allows people to see me the opposite of a leader will affect me adversely. Why? Because subconsciously, I will understand that I am messing up how I want to be remembered after I died. Therefore, I will NOT be successful. And if I can' t be successful, I can' t be happy. This is the same for you. Since I know how I want to be remembered, I treat people a certain way no matter what.

For those of you who are parents, you will have noticed that I don' t have "Good Father" on my list. I don't need to because the way you interpret success and happiness as far as *good father* is concerned, I do not. Let me explain. One of my biggest desires is for my kids to see me as a good leader, which is far more important to me, than for them to see me as just a father. I am what you would call a *servant leader*. Therefore, I have no choice but to be a good father because I don't get to be a good leader and miss their lives or their dreams, as a result, I homeschool my children. Where I go, they go. They get their education from me. I answer their 1 million questions in class and believe me; they have 1 million every time we bring up science. Since leadership is such a big deal for me, I have trained my kids to have high levels of confidence. They take

So Happy and Grateful

Antonio T.Smith, Jr

business classes with me, they take self-esteem classes with me and read self-help books with me. As of the release of this book, all my kids are less than ten years old. They know how to invest, and they truly believe that nothing is impossible. Here is what is important about this:

What is happiness for me has affected the way I raise my children. They don' t just get a birth father; they get a father who must be a good leader to them and for them. They must

*also see me treat my employees
as a good leader. It would crush
me   for   them   to   see   me
mistreating anyone that works
for me or works with me.*

This is the power of knowing what makes
you happy; as you write down what makes
you happy, it will work its way into
every area of your life. Every single
one. From this example, you can see how
*being a good parent in your way, and
then being a good parent in my way,* may
differ. However, we are both right. You
just wouldn't be fair if you tried to

put your parenting on me, nor would I be right if I told you to homeschool your kids and make them see you as a leader.

Wisdom From Brian Tracy

There are a few ingredients to happiness in which you need to be aware. Brian Tracy is a significant influence of the mind, and I think he captures this better than anyone I have ever seen or heard talk upon the subject. In the spirit of giving you the best information possible, I will quote his

7 Ingredients of Happiness [3] that I wish all of you will receive in the deepest parts of who you are.

1) Peace Of Mind

The first of these seven ingredients to a happy life, and easily the most important are peace of mind. It is the highest human good. Without it, nothing else has much value. Because of this, you strive for

---

[3]

https://www.briantracy.com/blog/personal-success/happy-life-self-improvement-positive-thinking/

So Happy and Grateful

Antonio T.Smith, Jr

it all your life. You usually evaluate how well you are doing at any given time by how much inner peace you enjoy.

Peace of mind and positive thinking is essential for the optimal performance and happy life of all human groupings, from your relationships with your friends and family to the business and organizations in which you work.

2) Health And Energy

The second ingredient to a happy life is health and energy. Just as peace of mind is your healthy and natural mental state, health and energy is your normal and natural physical state.

3) Loving Relationships
The third ingredient to a happy life, is loving relationships. These are relationships with people you love and care about, and the people who love and care about you. They are the real

measure of how you are doing as a human being. Happiness or unhappiness in life comes from your relationships with others, and it is your relationships with others that make you truly human.

4) Financial Freedom

, The fourth ingredient of a happy life and success, is economic freedom. To be financially free means that you have enough money so that you don ' t worry about it *continually, as most people do. It is not money that lies at the root of all evil; it is the lack of money. Achieving your financial freedom is one of the most important goals and responsibilities of your life. It is far too important to be left to chance.*

A feeling of economic freedom is essential to your self-improvement and the achievement of any other important goal, and you cannot be truly free until and unless you have enough money that you are no longer preoccupied with it.

5) Worthy Goals And Ideas
The fifth ingredient of a happy life is setting worthy goals and ideals. Perhaps your deepest subconscious drive, according to Dr. Viktor E. Frankl, author of Man's Search for Meaning, is the need for meaning and purpose in life. To be truly happy, you need a clear

sense of direction. You need
positive thinking to get there.
You need a commitment to
something bigger and greater
than yourself. You need to feel
that your life stands for
something, that you are somehow
making a valuable contribution
to the world.

Happiness has been defined
as " the progressive
realization of a worthy ideal. "
You can only be happy with
yourself when you are working

step by step toward something that is important to YOU.

6)   Self-Knowledge   And Self-Awareness

,   The   sixth   ingredient   to success and a happy life, is self-knowledge   and self-awareness. Throughout all of history, self-knowledge has gone hand in hand with inner happiness, positive thinking, and   outer   achievement.   To perform your best, you need to know who you are and why you

So Happy and Grateful

Antonio T.Smith, Jr

think and feel the way you do.

7) Personal Fulfillment
The seventh ingredient to a happy life is a sense of personal achievement. This is a feeling that you are becoming everything that you are moving toward in life. It is the realization of your full potential as a human being. Your happy life begins with self-improvement and ends with a personal fulfillment that you have accomplished all that you

wanted to.

In all honesty, I don't think I could have said this better, so quoting the great Brian Tracy is the safest move here. I want you to be transformed by this book. Your happiness is yours to keep, and also yours to protect. I will tell you this, if you are suffering in any of these areas, you are not receiving new information in these regions. The fix for you is straightforward, forget what you think you know in your deficient areas, and get you a coach, book or mentor in these areas and start winning. Allow something outside of your current level of awareness to change your levels of consciousness.

The Law of Integrity

If you read the right books or go to seminars such as Brian Tracy's and many others in the self-help field, you will discover the eight laws listed in the book that defines and explain the Laws of Happiness. The Law of Integrity is first. The law of integrity has three parts. The first is:

Happiness arises as a by-product of your choosing to live your life consistent with your highest values and aspirations

Okay, this one is easy to explain but also dangerous. Let me first give a disclaimer. I am going to tell you to trust your instincts and do what you know is right for you, but this does not refer to your "little mind," but the part of you that is tapped into infinite intelligence. You may call it your gut instinct, or your Holy Spirit, or anything in between. Either way, don't let your pride become an issue here. Most people would rather be right than in harmony when you fall into this category; you doom yourself to poverty. Being right is not important unless you are trying to be "right" concerning what is universal.

You are designed with an inner guide or consciousness. Think of it as your compass, the internal compass that guides us through life towards our supreme destiny. Every single time you go against this inner guide, you will have limited success, and immediately find yourself unhappy. Don't do this. Your goals and your values must be congruent with one another.

The best way for you to master this is to remember how you want to be remembered when you die. Go back to that exercise. How you want the people to speak to you when you have died is the truest form of your inner values. It is what drives you and keeps you up at night. To do anything that violates that list will make you unhappy and miserable people are always unsuccessful— even if they are rich and are considered to be successful.

To thine own self, be true. – William Shakespeare

The second part is:

Whenever you choose to live consistently with the very best that is in you, you will automatically experience happiness and joy.

Whenever you do what is best for you and give your best, you will always be happy. Even if you take a loss when you

So Happy and Grateful

Antonio T.Smith, Jr

have truly given your best you will be able to handle whatever comes next and be at peace with your decisions. There is a beautiful way I love to explain this in my seminars. "When leaving a relationship with a person you truly love, if you have not given your absolute best, you will never find complete peace with your decision. You will often run back and forth between who you want and who you left. However, when you believe that you have given your absolute best, you will find joy in your decision. Even if there is no real joy to be found— you will find comfort. Some sacred texts call this " peace that surpasses all understanding. "

It is super-important that you have done your very best in whatever you are doing. If you do not, you will not be happy. When you behave in a manner consistent with your highest values, you will feel valuable. When you do this, you will always see that everything will always work out in the end. Peace of mind should always be your highest goal. You deserve peace of mind. You can never make someone else happy when you are unhappy yourself.

So Happy and Grateful

Antonio T.Smith, Jr

Don't ever consistently sacrifice your happiness to give someone else theirs. No one will ever be pleased in this equation.

The third part is

When you set goals and ideas that are worthy of you, and you strive to achieve them, you will experience happiness and satisfaction.

Always remember, when you set a high bar for yourself and then hit that high bar, you will experience a level of happiness that most people on earth will never be able to achieve because they don't try to push themselves. My life moved into abundance when I decided to stop being 100% successful at hitting small targets and decided to have the courage to be 100% successful and being willing to die for the big targets that I set for myself. Believe me. I am one of the happiest people you will ever meet because I am always reaching a goal that I always knew that I could reach if I just tried harder than I ever did before. Every day you meet me you will meet me on a day in which I feel invincible. Which means,

So Happy and Grateful

Antonio T.Smith, Jr

every day you meet me you will have met me on the best day of my life! And that is worth every bit of the pain it takes for me to reach higher.

Adopt this attitude if you want to be happy.

So Happy and Grateful

Antonio T.Smith, Jr

Transformational Exercises

Defining Your Happiness

1. Defining Your Happiness as described in the *Funeral Exercise*

2. Based on your funeral exercise, write down what makes you happy in detail and developed a definite plan to obtain it.

3. Compare your list and detailed plan to the 7 Ingredients of Happiness.

So Happy and Grateful

Antonio T.Smith, Jr

If your list doesn't match the 7 Ingredients of Happiness, reconsider your list and detailed plan until it aligns with the 7 Ingredients of Happiness.

Finding Harmony With Happiness

1. Practice pausing before you speak or react that next time you are angered, offended, or feel that your intelligence has been insulted. Ask yourself the following questions:

• Do you have to be right at this moment?

• Will it benefit you to be right at this moment?

- Are you proving your point and not solving the problem? You cannot do both and have happiness.

- What did I do to cause the situation?

- Do you ever feel like you create any of your situations? If you do, do you have a habit of not admitting it out loud?

2. How can you make everyday people meet you the best day of your life?

Master Your Emotions

THE LAW OF EMOTION

Chapter 3

Why Aren't You Happy?

So Happy and Grateful

Antonio T.Smith, Jr

This is probably the most important chapter in this book. Lucky people are also rational people. However, reasonable doesn't mean to separate your decisions, although we would like to say that. Instead, it means to master your emotions during the decision-making process. Emotions are a blessing from the creative source, but they are a curse to the person who operates in a low level of awareness.

There was a time in your life that you couldn't imagine having your car, but now that you have it, you aren't happy. There was a time that you prayed to be married, but now that you are married, you aren' t happy. Why? You dreamed of having your place to stay, but now that you have it, you aren' t happy. Why? It is because you haven' t mastered your emotions.

Listen to me; you have survived every storm that has ever assaulted you in your life. You have survived every repossession of your happiness and your cars. You have survived over 100 of the worst days of your life, yet somehow, you are still not happy. This is not the way to live. Don' t be moved by exhaustion. Exhaustion is not your friend if you have not mastered your emotions. When one is exhausted and emotional, one will make the worst decisions possible. You have never made good decisions from bad emotional and mental places. Take notice, you can make good decisions from bad circumstances, but you cannot make good decisions if you are in a dangerous emotional and mental place.

Compassion Fatigue

You are a survivor, but you don't feel like it. When you are exhausted, you become fearful in safe places. It is called compassion fatigue. "Compassion Fatigue is a state experienced by those helping people or animals in distress; it is an extreme state of tension and preoccupation with the suffering of those being helped to the degree that it can create a secondary traumatic stress for the helper." Dr. Charles Figley. [1]

Caring too much can hurt. When caregivers focus on others without practicing self-care,

---

[1]

destructive behaviors can surface. Apathy, isolation, bottled up emotions and substance abuse head a long list of symptoms associated with the secondary traumatic stress disorder now labeled: Compassion Fatigue.

There is nothing more important than this moment right now. We all need to be reminded of this. Don't be moved by exhausted emotions. Frankly, when your emotions are exhausted, they will send you false signals. They will make you distrust people who love you. They will make you tired when you are full of energy. They will make you feel like you have no appetite when you haven' t eaten a single thing all day. When you get tired, you make dumb decisions, and there is no way to be happy when you are suffering from compassion fatigue. Don' t be moved by exhausted emotions. Here is an amazing TED Talk on *How to*

Manage Compassion Fatigue in Caregiving by Patricia Smith. [2]

What do you do when survival no longer feels like success? My friends, one of the most dangerous places to be on planet earth is between your breakdown and your breakthrough. There are so many opposing forces that will come to you when you are at this location. There are infinite possibilities of distractions that can come against you that will never allow

---

[2]

https://www.youtube.com/watch?v=7keppA8XRas

So Happy and Grateful

Antonio T.Smith, Jr

you to use the energy needed to get to your breakthrough. There is nothing wrong with being tired, but you have to learn how to master your emotions.

The Consequences of Being Unhappy

When you are tired, you cannot listen to your thoughts. When you are tired and try to fix your problems, you will only create more problems that you have to fix. You will isolate yourself and kill any chance you had of getting any right answers because you are filled with all the wrong answers. Don't be moved by exhausted emotions.

When you spend your life thinking that you can't make it when you can, you will find yourself very unhappy. You must learn that when you are not happy, it is tough to trust your decision-making paradigm. You will begin to lash out at people for no reason at all. You will lose your motivation to change your life. Being unhappy makes you fearful. Being unhappy takes the pleasure away from surviving. Being unhappy makes your perception of the joy in life and only allows you to focus on all the things that are keeping you miserable. Being unhappy will ruin all of your relationships and cause you to make the other party unhappy because you won't allow anything they do to make you happy.

When you are unhappy, you will deny yourself the right to be happy by any means necessary. Something wonderful will happen to you, and you will say things like, "It's not going to last long." When you say stuff like this, you become a killer-of-happiness. How many times have you been guilty of murdering your happiness and the happiness of others? When you live a life like this, anyone who is successful must avoid you because you are a ticking time bomb waiting to explode. When successful people are not in your life, you are no longer in the ebb and flow of what can make and keep you successful. And if you cannot be successful, you cannot be happy. Just because things are broken in your life doesn't mean you have to be sad! Don't waste your energy trying to fix things that will never come back to life.

So Happy and Grateful

Antonio T.Smith, Jr

When you are always unhappy, you will find joy in being unhappy, and confuse that with actual pleasure. You will post negative memes on social media and then get likes and comments, and that will give you joy. However, that is not real joy; it is just self-sabotaging masquerading itself as happiness.

When you are unhappy, you live in a constant state of being in love with what you had. This is one of the most dangerous things you can do to yourself. When you are constantly in love with what you had, you are constantly diminishing all the beautiful things that you have. Additionally, there can never be anything in your present that will ever add value to your life because all of your energy is being sent to the things you use to have. You will always talk about how good things used to be, instead of loving how things are now.

The Law of Emotion

Let's free you from this bondage. If you are free already, let's add value to your freedom. The Law of Emotion is a universal law that you need to master quickly. The Law of Emotion states:

Human beings are 100% emotional in everything they think, feel, and decide.

Although very rational and logical people like me would love to tell you that we are 90% logical and 10% emotional when it comes to decision-making, this is false. Both research and science have proven that people are entirely emotional in everything that they do. I know. It's an ego killer to find out that you have been emotional all this time, but it is true. Even if you are 99% rational like me, you are emotional about being rational, and that rationale comes from an emotional place. You are only rational because you have been hurt by not being rational in the past and being rational in your present is simply an emotional reaction that now rewards you. The moment you are no longer rewarded for being rational, you will then change how you approach those situations that do not reward you, and you will adjust your plan. Don't believe me, try getting married or getting into a long-term relationship and see how much you get rewarded for always being rational when you should have been emotional. Humans change any behaviors that do not reward them. This makes us all emotional. Even if we think it is simply a logical decision to make. We make that logical decision because we are all trying to move towards happiness. Therefore, we are all emotional. Logical simply means you have more emotions into that course of action than you do any others.

The first part of the Law of Emotion is:

So Happy and Grateful

Antonio T.Smith, Jr

You are motivated by two major types of emotions, those of love or desire and those of fear or loss.

You know these emotions as positive emotions and negative emotions. Think of these as Sigmund Freud did: these are feelings of pleasure and pain. Everyone is always moving towards those experiences that give them pleasure, or happiness, and away from those that give them pain, or unhappiness. Be careful with interpreting this, because some of you have self-esteem so low that what gives you pleasure is to self-sabotage and hurt yourself. As a result, you will always be moving towards what hurts you because you have convinced yourself that you aren' t worth anything that all, and it gives you secret joy to prove yourself right so you can always have other people to blame for the failures in your life.

The second law of emotion explains:

The content of your emotional life is largely determined by the thoughts you dwell upon most of the time.

This goes back to the very last sentence I wrote about the first part of the Law of Emotion. "As a result, you will always be moving towards what hurts you because you have convinced yourself that you aren't worth anything that all, and it gives you secret joy to prove yourself right so you can always have other people to blame for the failures in your life. " You may have heard of this being referred to as your " dominate thoughts". You are always drifting in life to what you are predominately thinking. If you think you are worthless, you will always manifest in your life people and circumstances that will create more of the feeling of being worthless. As far as the Law of Emotion is concerned, since no one ever wants to be proved wrong, your secret desire is always to be right about the things you know. Therefore, it makes you happy to be in pain in this scenario because your dominate thoughts must move you towards suffering. As a result, you keep drifting towards pain because that pain is secretly pleasing to you — which ultimately proves Sigmund Freud correct. You keep moving towards your pleasure, even if that desire keeps you in pain. Think of it as a drug addiction. Except, in this case, you are addicted to depression, which is neurologically possible and correct. Depression produces certain hormones, and your body becomes addicted to that hormone.

In short, if you think angry thoughts, you will be an angry person. If you think sad thoughts, you will be a sad person— and so on, and so on. It

So Happy and Grateful

Antonio T.Smith, Jr

is probably best for your future and health to think happy thoughts. That way, by the Law of Emotion, you have to be a happy person.

The third part of the Law of Emotion is:

If you deliberately choose to think positive, loving, uplifting thoughts, you can create and maintain your happiness in spite of what is happening around you.

I explain this to people I coach as *take responsibility for your energy.* No one can make you unhappy but you. If you allow them to make you miserable, the fault is always yours, because you have the power over you— no one else. No one can make you feel unhappy without your consent. Therefore, the smartest thing you can ever do for yourself is to choose what kind of thoughts you want to have in your head and this law will move you towards that direction.

Transformational Exercises

Mastering Your Emotions

1. Separate the facts of your situations from how you feel about the situation.

2. If you feel your feelings are correct, ask someone not involved in the situation if they are. If you can't find a trustworthy, find a motivational speech or coaching

session online that speaks on your situation, or read a book about handling your situation.

3. If you are tired, don't make significant decisions. Rest and relax, even if for a short period.

Letting Go of Dead Situations That You Are Keeping Alive

1. Evaluate all your emotional struggles. Review all facts until there is zero confusion or as little confusion as possible.

2. Write on a piece of paper of all the things you have not forgiven or still or angered by in great detail and

then burn that piece of paper. Watch every bit of the paper be consumed and allow everything you wrote on the paper to disappear in the fire.

3. For the next 24 hours, every time you see something that you were able to buy at any point in your life, say thank for it— no matter how old, small, or insignificant.

4. For the next 48 hours, say thanks for the things you have that you could never buy and were freely given by the universe. Such as, but not limited to, your sight, your children, your lungs, your health, your parents, your peace

So Happy and Grateful

Antonio T.Smith, Jr

of mind, your life, your future abundance, and more.

5. Identify how much you self-sabotage yourself, your happiness, and your relationships.

6. Write down how many times today has someone or some situations caused you to be unhappy, and force yourself to admit that you gave away your permission to be happy.

7. Throughout the day, list decisions you have made to make other people happy knowing that your decision would make your miserable.

Be Your Own Hero

THE LAW OF HAPPINESS

CHAPTER 4

Being Your Own Hero

So Happy and Grateful

Antonio T.Smith, Jr

It is nice to treat people the way you want to be treated and to treat them better than you want to be treated because that is how you take your rightful place in this world. Some people will say this is for religious purposes, but truthfully this is just how the universe is aligned. As stated in chapter one, this book has no religious undertone, but only deals with what is universal. Quantum entanglement is thought to be one of the trickiest concepts in science, but

the core issues are simple[1]. I won't go into
entanglement in this book, but a simple explication
would be since everything in the universe came from
one place and was all connected at the beginning of
time, we are still all connected to this day. This
pertains to all things, not just humans— all things. So,
you have a responsibility to be kind to everything in
this world.

It is time for you to be your own
hero. You are hero material, and you
have to permit yourself to save
yourself. Of course, you can' t protect

---

[1]

https://www. quantamagaz
ine. org/entanglement-made
-simple-20160428/

So Happy and Grateful

Antonio T.Smith, Jr

yourself when you consistently deny the opportunity to look at yourself. You are amazing. Period! Receive this compliment and become your hero. It is up to you to see yourself as a hero.

The time to enjoy yourself is now. As soon as you open your eyes in the morning, you deserve to be happy. You have the power to steer your thoughts and emotions in the direction that you want them to go and not the direction they want to go. You are a being of unlimited power, and it is time to make yourself feel good. Obviously, I don't mean rob banks or become reckless.

This wouldn't make sense because we are all connected, and whatever you do to one of us, you do to all of us.

Gratitude Is the Most Powerful Connection

You have to make a choice. Seize the day or let the day conquer you. What did you decide this morning? Too many people focus on the "how" of a problem instead of being grateful for the opportunity to have a problem. This is why there are very few individuals in this world who achieve abundance.

So Happy and Grateful

Antonio T.Smith, Jr

There is humor all around you, be grateful for it. Even if you cannot see yourself past your pain, there is still humor around you. The more you focus on your lack, the more you are going to get that lack back. Don't put your happiness on hold for another moment. What will you accomplish today and how grateful will you be? Better yet, what if you woke up this morning with just the things you said thank you for yesterday? How much would you have today? Would your children be alive? Your parents? You?

So Happy and Grateful

Antonio T.Smith, Jr

Gratitude is the most powerful connection that you have to your higher self, and you should always live this life operating in your higher mind— your big mind. Don' t entertain those little thoughts that come from fearful places. When was the last time that you included you in your own life? So many people include everyone else in their lives but never bother to include themselves. The time to enjoy yourself is right now.

You determine whether you are going to enjoy the day, not outside circumstances. You create your reality, and your entire life is based on the choices that you make. Choose to live the quality of life that is worthy of you. Being happy doesn' t mean that you are exempt from the pain of life. It just means that you will bounce back to normal faster than others. Bless this life with your smile. It' s a wonderful world, smile at it.

The thoughts that you have about the quality of your life will be exactly what you live throughout that life. You are creating the world you are happy about and the world you are complaining about as well. If there is anything that is going to keep you from being successful in life, it is the way you talk to yourself. The whole world is yours for the taking. Sometimes you are the problem, and I want you to let this issue go. Be grateful. Build your dreams by enjoying this current moment. Look at how many words you have read so far. Do you know how many people can't read? You are doing better than them. Be grateful.

The Law of Happiness

The Law of Happiness states:

The quality of your life is
largely determined by how you
feel at any given moment.

This quote is so accurate. You are only as happy as you feel. You will only enjoy things to the level of your mood. If you can construct your belief system and begin to let a good feeling find its way into your actions, you will win! Life is about facing your fears and facing your fears taking discipline. Those who have discipline have made it a habit of taking the hard road that makes them better in life. It is so easy to be angry all the time. It is super easy to blame others. Discipline is not punishment. Discipline is the rent you pay for future abundance.

How you feel will determine your level of energy, the quality of your relationships. It is the process that will determine your happiness. Enjoy the process. "There may be people who have more talent than you, but there is no excuse for anyone to work harder than you." These are the wise words of Derek Jeter. News flash, you can't work hard when you feel bad all the time.

So Happy and Grateful

Antonio T.Smith, Jr

The first part of the Law of Happiness is:

How you feel, the quality of your emotional life, is largely determined by how you talk to yourself.

You criticize you more than you will ever criticize others. At least, this is true for most people. Two of the most powerful words on the planet is "I am"; therefore, whatever you put after "I am" will come follow you without limits. If you say, "I am stupid," stupidity will come and follow you without limits. If you say, " I am broke, " poverty will come and follow you without limits. " I am " is an invitation to whatever comes after those words. Watch how you talk to yourself. You are not fat. You are releasing the weight you don't need. You are not broke. You are standing in the middle of money. There is nothing average about you. There will never be another you, and you are beautiful.

If you change your self talk, your life will go to another level. It is up to you how you talk to yourself, but I want to encourage you never to say anything negative about yourself, especially when you are joking. When you jokingly talk negatively about yourself, you permit yourself to add extra energy to negative self-talk. Don't do it. Change your self-talk.

The second part of the Law of Happiness is:

The way you interpret events to yourself determines your emotional response to those events.

Yeah, your perception is killing you or making you wealthy. One or the other, but there is not in between. My mentor, Les Brown says it best, "There are winners, and there are losers, and then there are people who haven't quite yet figured out how to win." Individuals with a poor perception tend to fall into this third category. They have the brains and talent of successful people, but their attitude controls their responses to events. How you react to what happens to you is how you will manifest that event in the future. You will always plant how you feel.

The third part of the Law of Happiness is:

So Happy and Grateful

Antonio T.Smith, Jr

The fastest way to take control of your emotions is to look for the good in any given situation you are facing.

This is where I typically get beat up, metaphorically, of course, when I am coaching people. They can't possibly believe that it is good in all of their bad situations. There truly is. Anytime failure arises in your life, use your perception to recognize that failure holds all the keys you need to the breakthrough you want. Winning never comes to us as cute gold medals.

So Happy and Grateful

Antonio T.Smith, Jr

It comes to us as four years of hard practice and strict diets. We don't just get to take the gold medal home. We have to work for years for it and pass up on all the food we want to eat to get the gold medal we desire. This will always be a fact. Whether you want it to be or not.

So Happy and Grateful

Antonio T.Smith, Jr

Transformational Exercises

Creating A Day of Winning

1. Examine all the people you see or interact with consistently, and list all the things you have in common with one another.

2. Make the first 5-minutes all about saying thank you. In the next 5 minutes, only visualize yourself winning at everything you need to

accomplish today and leave your house expecting to receive 100% victories throughout your day.

3. Do something today that no-one else can do better than you.

4. Ask yourself, "How would the future-successful version of me do what I am about to do next?"

5. Create a to-do list for the day and monitor how much you accomplished. If you did not accomplish 100% of your to-do list, learn how to prioritize what is most important for your future abundance, and make sure you accomplish all of your tasks.

So Happy and Grateful

Antonio T.Smith, Jr

6. Create 10 "I am" statements that will immediately impact both your present and your future. Repeat them aloud, twice daily until you receive what you have written.

7. From this moment forth, become highly aware that you also plant what you feel, not just what you consciously plant.

The Switcharoo

THE LAW OF SUBSTITUTION

CHAPTER 5

The fourth law of happiness states:

You can keep yourself positive by substituting a positive thought for a negative thought.

So Happy and Grateful

Antonio T.Smith, Jr

If you listen and take evasive action, I can help you change your future. I wish someone would have told me this decades ago, but they didn't. So, I will now say it to you. It is simple. It is not catchy, but it is profound.

You don't have to be sad.

I know, simple. That doesn't make it lose its power. You do not have to be sad. Sadly is not normal. It feels healthy, but you were not a sad fetus, nor were you unhappy baby. You nearly came out smiling, and someone of you even cracked a smile within your first day of living.

When you are in a bad spot, you become sad for so long that you convince yourself that is how you are supposed to feel. It is not. You are stronger than that. As humans, we want to find out what it is like to be someone else and when you are reminded that you can' t be that someone, you get angry. You already knew that you couldn' t be anyone but you, but you convinced yourself that it was possible.

So Happy and Grateful

Antonio T.Smith, Jr

After years of repetitive sadness, you will need to rebuild your life by restoring your courage and your belief systems. You will have to do this for yourself. The moment you do it for someone else, you fail when they don't support you the way you think they should. When you place your happiness in their hands, they will let you down every time, no matter how much you love them and they love you. You must rebuild your life for yourself.

We are all dying, but only a small select few are living. You were meant for more. You were meant for greatness.

So Happy and Grateful

Antonio T.Smith, Jr

You can do this, and if you want to be the best, it is time for you to become obsessed with self-development. You can't shortchange yourself because you are only cheating yourself. Never give up. The world needs you now more than ever. If there is no joy when you wake up in the morning, you have work to do, but the work is possible. This will take effort! You will never see greatness without effort! You will need to be happy without effort!

So Happy and Grateful

Antonio T.Smith, Jr

A Stern Message

It is far too easy to blame everything and everybody for what you have going on with your life. Things do get rough, and sometimes you can't get a break, but that has nothing to do with your response to these events. You are a winner, even if you haven't learned how to win. There is a winner in you; your loser is just louder. Don't be lazy, be a warrior. You are the reason you are successful or not successful. You are the reason your surroundings are beautiful or dysfunctional. You can be in the hood living a peaceful life or in the suburbs living a terrible life. The choice is yours. No one is exempt from pain, and no one is free from joy. You get to decide which one of these emotions will dominate your life. You have every excuse in the world to fail or to succeed, but do remember this: *excuses only sound good to the people who are making them up.* No one else cares why you can't accomplish what you said you were going to accomplish. Wake up! If you are winning, wake up and start learning again, because winning will only teach you how to be comfortable and comfortable people lose. You will always be the reason why you are not winning or why you are winning.

The Law of Substitution

The next time you get a bad thought infiltrates your mind, replace it with an equal positive thought. Take massive action towards the things you want by replacing your negative thoughts.

You can win when you decide to take control of your thoughts. Of course, it is too hard to monitor all of your thoughts, but the ones that make you feel bad are worth replacing. You will only live your dominant thoughts, and those things can be sneaky.

Everything happens in your mind. Change your thoughts, and it will change your life. Break that negative spirit and make this life bow down to you. Tell those negative thoughts nothing. Don't give them energy and if you have to give them energy, only give them positive energy. Win! Win! Win! That is your job. Don't be determined to be negative. Be determined to be happy! This chapter isn't meant to tear you down and attribute to your negativity. It is designed to be short and to kick you in the butt if you need it. Everything about your life is what you have decided to live. The outcome of your life and your career is based on the choices that you have made.

So Happy and Grateful

Antonio T.Smith, Jr

Transformational Exercises

Switching Your Luck

This book comes with a free self-development course with hours of additional audio content, training, and more. It will help with this Switcharoo process. Access it from www.antoniotsmithjr.com/so-happy-and -grateful

I love you.

Earth Vs. The Real World

THE LAW OF EXPRESSION

CHAPTER 6

The Fifth Law of happiness states:

Whatever is expressed is impressed and whatever is impressed is expressed.

Happiness And The Willingness To Die

What dream or vision do you want to turn into a reality? Because, without joy, it will be near impossible to accomplish. You can dream of any life you want, but happiness, a plan, and unfailing belief in the obtainment of your dream are the only things that can make that dream become a reality. Success is a campaign. It is not a one-and-done type of stuff. You must be willing to die for your dream and be willing to live in happiness while you are ready to die for it. There is no other way to live your dream. To live out a dream is to be willing to die for it while being happy that you have the opportunity to do so. Period. There is no other way. The person who is ready to be happy the most is the person who will be able to bounce back from failures the most. People are not perfect, but happiness makes them okay with that fact.

There is no hack to happiness. Happiness is a hard journey that rewards those who dare to travel it brilliantly. Those who are super successful are those who have become obsessed with being happy. Every day should be the best day of your life, even when you are in the middle of a bad day. I feel very strongly that we are who we choose to be. There is nothing that you can tell me differently about this because I understand the science behind consciousness creating reality. Nothing can come into your reality until you *observe it*. This will be very hard to accept if you have a victim mentality, but it is true. Wherever your energy goes, that thing will grow. Whatever you look at in your mind, you will eventually look at in your hand. The person who is willing to observe happiness will also hold happiness.

If you are focused, and passionate, and driven, you will get anything you want in life, because your happiness will attract it or make you figure it out. We have control of our minute, our hour, our day, our week, our month, and our year. Stop letting people put things on you that don't serve you

So Happy and Grateful

Antonio T.Smith, Jr

during any of these periods. Don't allow people to keep you in discomfort so they can be comfortable. Honestly, most of you are surrounded by individuals who are only comfortable with your presence when you are uncomfortable in theirs. Do you expect your life to be different when you hang around these types of people? Does that reflect an individual who loves themselves? Do you reflect an individual who loves yourself? Being alone is not bad unless you don't want to be alone. Being around people is not a bad thing unless you want to be alone.

So Happy and Grateful

Antonio T.Smith, Jr

There is nothing in this world that matters except for the world that exists inside your head. It is the world inside your mind that determines the things that will appear in the world outside of your mind. So, in actuality, the real world is not the world you experience out here, but the world you create in there.

Watch The People Around You

The individuals who are included your day are the people you believe you *deserve* to have included in your day.

Change your mind, and it will change your life. If you can't change your thoughts because the things around you are bad, then change the things around you by leaving them so that you can change your mind. Life is too short to be in a relationship that doesn't serve you. You have to break through that negative energy to get to the positive life. All of that garbage that you are carrying is keeping you from getting to your dreams. Dreams are afraid of garbage. If they see you taking garbage, they will flee from you because you are holding on to what scares them. Don' t be determined to be miserable. If you don't think you are determined to be miserable, here is a test that can help you see past your vision into the truth. Ask yourself if the people around you are sad. If they are miserable then so are you, because like attracts like.

Your job is to feel good about the people around you. Just because they grew up with you doesn't mean they have to travel to success with you. Everyone you love isn't meant for the travel — you will have to come back for them when you get yourself out of poverty. Dysfunction will keep successful

So Happy and Grateful

Antonio T.Smith, Jr

people away from you, and you need successful people to put in a word for you. Decide today that you are worthy of being happy.

The Law of Expression

Whatever is expressed is impressed and whatever is impressed is expressed.

Your thoughts are not your own, and your actions come from your mind. Most of you are only behaving a certain way because someone has taught you how to respond when a particular event occurs.

You have been taught how to respond when someone has an affair, when your bank account has a specific number in it, and when someone lies to you. All of your responses have been taught to you by people who had a considerable amount of influence over you. Today, you respond to events and circumstances almost exactly how you were taught to respond. The question now becomes, were those people successful and did they teach you how to respond successfully. If racism has to be taught, you must also have to

So Happy and Grateful

Antonio T.Smith, Jr

respect that poverty must also be taught.

Transformational Exercises

Creating Your New World

1. Go to a quiet spot, perhaps in bed at night. Close your eyes and repeat aloud so you may hear your own words the written statement of the new world you desire to have for yourself, the time limit for its manifestation, and a description of the service and sacrifice you intend to give in return

for this new world. As you carry out these instructions, see yourself already living in the happiness and abundance of this new world.

Example

By the first day of xxx, my life will look like xxx. This life will come to me in various manners, and I will be open to receive this new life, even when it doesn't t come in the manner in which I expect.

In return for this new life and amazing level of happiness, I will give the most efficient service of which I am capable of rendering the fullest possible quantity, and the best possible quality of service in the capacity of xxx.

I believe that I will have this new life in my possession. My faith is so strong that I can now see how happy I am in it right now. I can hold this new life in my heart and–and my hands. I have the exact car and house that I want. I have the type of love that I want. I have the exact level of health that I need to enjoy it all long term. This new life is now awaiting transfer to me at the time, and in the proportion that I

So Happy and Grateful

Antonio T.Smith, Jr

deliver the service, I intend to render in return for it.

I have a plan by which to obtain and live in this new life, and I will follow that plan with a burning desire and unwavering persistence regardless of obstacles.

2. Repeat this program night and morning until you can see in your imagination the new life that you have created for yourself.

3. Place a written copy of your statement where you can see it night and morning and read it just before

retiring and upon arising until it's been memorized.

Tricking Your Brain

THE LAW OF REVERSIBILITY

CHAPTER 7

The Sixth Law of Happiness states:

So Happy and Grateful

Antonio T.Smith, Jr

Just as your feelings determine your actions, your actions determine your feelings.

There is a wonderful way to explain this. It is called *fake it until you make it*. You can use your actions to change your feelings. We have all had setbacks, disappointments, and hurt feelings. You cannot live a victorious life when you are always looking back and reliving the negative things that have happened to you. When people hurt you, and you keep reliving it, you allow them to hurt you again and again, because you won't focus on anything else.

Things You Can Do To Reverse Your Sadness

When you pretend that you have positive feelings, you will send to your brain, in reverse, how it should be responding. Take this for example. If you are depressed, hurt, having a bad day, and you go outside to run, you will tell your brain, "Hey brain. We aren't upset. We aren't sad; we are so happy we are moving forward." The simple act of running will force your brain to send different signals to your body that will immediately alter your mood.

When you are feeling sad, say thank you over and over. Stand up and look around your house and for every item that you see, say thank you for it. Every time you see something, say thank you and your mind will get the signal that you are no longer sad. It will then force your body to match the meaning of the word "thank you," and you will immediately alter your mood.

Get up and get it done. Be remarkable because you were born to be. Don't ask anyone for permission. Just get up and get the next step to your dreams done. Don't take today off. You have 24 hours a day, which means your success is dependent on how you use the 24 hours. Use them wisely and go to sleep tonight with absolutely zero energy. Don't prove the people who want you to fail right and prove the few people who do believe in you wrong. You are worth your dream!

Just as your feelings determine your actions, your actions determine your feelings.

So Happy and Grateful

Antonio T.Smith, Jr

Practicing positive self-talk will help you raise your self-esteem, significantly, and help you to focus on your strengths rather than flaws and weaknesses. Your flaws are your flaws — keep them that way. To be successful, you have to double down on what you are good at and let other people do what you do not do well. You can reverse your sadness by talking to yourself in a better manner.

Do yourself a favor and practiced balanced thinking. This means when you come up with a plan, plan for all the amazing things to happen and then think out all the equal bad things that can happen. Not only will this improve your plan, it will also keep your happier when bad things do happen. Small and steady will always win the race.

Small daily improvements over time will lead you to stunning results. Working hard is the cost of entry to anything. It is tough to work hard when you are sad. You can reverse engineer your happiness by using your actions to trick your mind into winning. Everything is connected, to include your actions with your mind and your mind with your actions.

So Happy and Grateful

Antonio T.Smith, Jr

Transformational Exercises

Releasing People Who Have Hurt You

Follow these steps to release the people who have hurt you and are stopping you from being happy.

Step 1 – Accept Who They Are

Some people are just some people, they will never change, at least not towards you. This is okay. Don't try to change them any longer. Accept all of who they are.

Step 2 – They Did The Best They Could With What They Had

Although this is a bit hard to accept at first, people typically do their best, sometimes their best just doesn' t serve you. This is okay. There is no sense in holding on to how they didn' t treat you right any longer. Accept that whatever they have, you received their best and that their best just wasn' t what you needed or what you deserved.

Step 3 – Release Them

To release does not mean to hate, but to simply let them go so you can be happy. Allow these people to go love or bother someone else in the universe. They have served their time and purpose in your life.

Step 4 – Move Forward

All of this was for nothing if you don't move forward in your own happiness. You are the most important thing to you, not the pain you held on to before this book.

The Body Follows The Mind

THE LAW OF VISUALIZATION

CHAPTER 8

The Seventh Law of Happiness says:

So Happy and Grateful

Antonio T.Smith, Jr

Ideas and images tend to awaken emotions and feelings that correspond to them.

Sometimes you can try so hard at something and still fail. This will most certainly cause some degree of disappointment, but failing is not the last step, unless you your mind has gone to that failure and stayed there. If not, you get up, you brush yourself off, you move forward, and you decide that you can't be stopped. You need to learn how to see difficulty differently. The next time you see it, push through it! Push! That is what you should, and you should do it often.

Unfortunately, this is not easy, and you will never be able to do it without the Law of Visualization. A person's character is not judged by how well they react during the good times, but how well they behave in the bad. Don't ever stop! You are either committed to prosperity or committed to poverty. There is no *between*, but most of you are living life in it while thinking it is safe. The middle is not safe. The middle is an illusion.

So Happy and Grateful

Antonio T.Smith, Jr

Your journey will not be easy. There will be times in which you will want to quit. You will feel this way, but you can never do anything unless your mind does it first. It is about this I want to talk to you.

To change your life it is not enough to simply hope that your life will change. You have to envision your life changing. You have to see it, and then believe it, and then receive it. Clarity is power. The more clear you are on what you want, the faster your brain can get you there. Achieve the outcome by taking your mind to the finish line first. When you get better, everything will get better for you, but you can only get better when you take your mind to a place that is already better. You must see your change in your mind before you can achieve it with your body.

A Word of Caution

Seeing where you want to go has nothing to do with *how*. The Law of Visualization is not about seeing how, but seeing what. *How* is not your responsibility. All you have to do is hold your goal before you, and everything else will take care of itself. Your goal is already yours because you had the power to think of it. It is already on its way because you put positive feelings with it. However, you will only obtain it when you see yourself receiving it and experience all the emotions of a receiver. Forget how. See yourself in the what.

So Happy and Grateful

Antonio T.Smith, Jr

The Visualization Process

Using visualization techniques to focus on your goals and desires accomplishes four essential things.

It activates your creative subconscious which will start generating creative ideas to achieve your goal.

When you take your mind out to the end goal— to the celebration of what you have not yet achieved, your mind will begin to build backward and figure out how to get there. It cannot understand that it has not been there. Your subconscious will begin to develop a plan for you to get where it just left from.

It programs your brain to more readily perceive and recognize the resources you will need to achieve your dreams.

As you back-build your dreams, your subconscious will begin to think of all the resources that you will need to obtain this final result. If you do not have the resources, it will develop a plan to get you to the resources that already exist. If the reason does not exist, your subconscious will then go into "inventor" mode and begin to create a new technology or resource that the world has yet to see, for you to obtain what you have just visualized.

It activates the law of attraction, thereby drawing into your life the people, resources, and circumstances you will need to achieve your goals.

When you use the visualization process, you will begin to vibrate at the same frequency of the end goal and then draw unto you all the things that match that frequency. These things and people will then assist you in getting to where your mind has visualized.

It builds your internal motivation to take the necessary actions to achieve your dreams.

Once you see what is possible, you will be fired up, if your happiness level is above average. If not, you won't be fired up, but intimidated. So, don't go through life holding back. Go

through this life-giving it every
single thing you have in you.

So Happy and Grateful

Antonio T.Smith, Jr

Transformational Exercises

Getting Your Mind Out The Middle

Write down everything you are struggling with and make a decision to move through that problem without stopping. Also, force yourself to admit that your middle is NOT prosperity. It is the only comfort, and there is very little abundance in comfort, and there is only false happiness in comfort.

So Happy and Grateful

Antonio T.Smith, Jr

Repetition Becomes Your Position

THE LAW OF PRACTICE

CHAPTER 9

The Eighth Law of Happiness states:

So Happy and Grateful

Antonio T.Smith, Jr

Whatever mental or physical activities you repeat and reinforce often enough become new habits of thought and behavior that eventually become automatic and unconscious.

Habits can make you, but they can also break you. You become what you think about most, but your legacy will always be what you have done the most. If you don't know where you are going, you will end up someplace else. If you don' t have a clear goal, you will fail every time.

Whatever you are repeating in your mind, you are creating in your world. Whatever you are repeating, that is what you are becoming a genius at doing. If you have a habit of being lazy, you will become a genius at being lazy. You will always be what you do consistently.

When you don't feel like doing something, that is exactly what you should be doing, because you will never feel like doing the right thing. Those things that cause us to be successful are annoying and take a lot of hard work. They make us uncomfortable. This is why you will never, ever feel like doing it. And that is why every time you feel like you don't want to do something, that is exactly what you want to do.

Winners Do This

When winners don't feel like doing something, they do it. When winners feel like taking a break, they don't. When winners write a blog, they make it a book. When winners have a lot to do, they prioritize. Winners chase their dreams and let losers hunt fun on weekends.

Anyone who is successful is obsessed with being successful. Winners go to seminars. How many have you attended this year? Winners read books. How many have you read this year? Winners don't wait to win, they win. Winners don't do, they dominate!

The Law of Practice is what winners understand will make them super successful. Motivation is nothing without action. You will always be motivated, but motivation is not enough to make you do. Discomfort or pleasure are the only two things that will get you to do anything.

It is the little things that will improve your life. Those little things that you thought were not important. We all have a habit of hesitating. So, don' t hesitate. Move! You have to move and move the moment you get an inspired idea, or your brain will figure out a way to make you not do what you need to do to be successful.

Additionally

The Law of Practice states that as you continue to practice and work on developing key skill areas, you will subsequently reduce the time required to perform certain tasks, which effectively increases your output and boosts your levels of productivity. In other words, you become very good at things that you once were not because repetition made you a boss!

What are you trying to dominate? Are you trying to dominate? The truth is, we all dominate in something. Most

people are just dominant at being sad
and average.

Transformational Exercises

Be Honest About Your Current Harvest

Ask yourself, "What is the most abundant thing in my life right now?", such as comfort, money, relationship problems, sadness, etc. When you identify the top 3 most abundant things in your life, you will also determine the type of seeds you are planting. These seeds can only be planted by what you think. It too difficult to monitor all your thoughts, but your dominant thoughts will always lead to a harvest. Track your harvest, you track your thoughts. If you have a harvest that doesn ' t serve your dreams, stop repeating those practices. Instead, practice new-seed-planting, and repeat that process.

The Law of Attraction

THE ONE LAW TO RULE THEM ALL

Chapter 10

The next three chapters: ten, eleven, and twelve, are going to be over the same subject, which is the law of the attraction. With certainty, most of you would have heard about the law of attraction at least once in your life, but what has been lost on most of you is that you have always applied the law of attraction. This is true with all people, through all lifetimes, and through all ages. The challenge I will have with some of you is proving that the law of attraction is real, which actually won't be hard at all because the law of attraction is a definite science. We will get to this in a moment. Another challenge I will have with some of you is convincing you that you have always used the law of attraction, even has a child. It is quite possible that my biggest challenge in this chapter will be to prove that you have manifested everything in your life— good or bad, and you are must account for this fact. Concurrently, I will move to proving to you that you can uncreate any reality in your life that you do not desire, by simply creating what you want. As a result, I will spend the last three chapters of the *Happiness Chapters* teaching you how to properly apply the law of attraction and its sister components.

So Happy and Grateful

Antonio T.Smith, Jr

Allow me to begin by telling all of you that *everything in your life is worth it.* It always has been and always will be. In short, life is always working for you and not to you. The trick to understanding all of this is for you to come to grips with the fact that you are a master creator and you —have created everything you are currently complaining about as well. There is a key concept that I will introduce to you now and I will expound on this concept in great detail later in Chapter 27. This concept is: *There is no such thing as lack.* Lack cannot exist in the universe unless man creates lack with his rules, arrogance, and ignorance. There is no lack. There are no problems to solve because every problem to solve has already been solved. There is no money for you to make because all the money has already been made. Everything already exists and you simply have to invoke the experience of what you desire to exist in *your* reality.

Anything in your current reality first caught your attention before it was there. Before you could have manifested it in your reality, on some level in your mind, you were keenly aware of what I am calling "anything" and then you manifested it into your reality. I will fully explain just how this has come to be in your life in the next chapter, but for now do your best to accept that your reality is a result of your awareness.

There are some confusing things about the law of attraction that we need to clear up before we dive into the deep waters of this chapter. First, let us, you and I, gain the understanding that you were already *in vibration* before you manifested the things in your reality. In reality, pun intended, your physical reality is simply the things that match your internal vibration.

The Law of Vibration

Here is a good starting point. The law of attraction is simply a side effect of the law of vibration. I don't know anyone non-scientist who explains the law of vibration better than Bob Proctor, philosopher and motivational speaker— and star of the movie *The Secret* was released in 2006. Bob

Proctor explains the law of vibration this way:

> " The underlying law that regulates supply in the world of effects has two important faces: one is desire and the other is expectation··· When we desire something we are instantly connected with the invisible side of whatever good we desire. It's expectation that reels it in. The Law of Attraction is not the primary law. The Law of Vibration is the

primary law. You see, everything in the universe vibrates. We literally live in an ocean of motion··· Nothing is resting. Everything is moving ··· Our brain is an electronic switching station, and our thoughts activate brain cells and control the vibration we' re in, and the vibration we' re in controls what we attract into our life. "

This is a lot to take in and you may even have to read it multiple times. I wish

I could quote to you exactly where Proctor has mentioned this quote, but he says it so often it is in multiple places. He has a series of messages called *The Eleven Lost Laws*, you will most certainly hear it on there, should you desire to check my sources. Nevertheless, if I had to explain this to my kids, I would simply say,

" Buddies, (this is what I affectionally call my two boys), the both of you have desires, but you also have expectations. Although you desire certain

things, it is your expectation that actually has the stronger vibration and you will then attraction your expectation of your desire *and not your desire. You will effectively get in life how you feel and now what you want, because your feelings are vibrations and everything in this world is vibrating. As you feel, buddies, your feelings will go out into this world and find the things that are vibrating at the exact frequency of your feelings and magnetize these thing back to the source of vibration, which is you. Therefore, you get what you feel or expect, not what you think buddies".*

This is how I would explain it to my two boys and this is how I explain it to you. I also have a little girl, she is very young in age and can be classified as an infant or a toddler, and she doesn' t have the cognitive ability to understand such a conversation yet, but the law of attraction doesn' t need her to understand words in order to manifest thing into her reality, it will just do so. She will get what she feels, whether she is conscious of this or not. For some of you, this is hard to except, especially if you have had traumatic childhoods. This is why parents are so important. When my daughter cries in anger about something she did not get, it is my job to communicate with her and make her feel better about the situation. It is my job every day to work on her confidence before she is gains the vocabulary word *confidence*. The more confidence I help her receive as a

So Happy and Grateful

Antonio T.Smith, Jr

child, the more she will be able to wield the law of attraction for things that serve her. I have used my children here as a guide for those who can understand and for those who cannot. The law of attraction will work in your lives regardless of your understanding or your level of belief.

When you find vibrational alignment for a long period of time, the bumps and bruises of life won't affect you as much as others will be affected. When you become a creator of your own reality, while others are feeling the pains of recessions and

So Happy and Grateful

Antonio T.Smith, Jr

economic downturns, you will experience prosperity. The goal of learning the law of attraction is for you to be able to go around anyone, anywhere, and maintain all the good things you are attracted into your life. Essentially, you will draw unto you all the good that you desire whoever you go and whoever you find yourself with— regardless of the circumstances. Make sure that you get to the level of belief that you are one big vibration and you are always calling into your life the things that match your vibration.

So Happy and Grateful

Antonio T.Smith, Jr

Deeper Into The Law of Vibration

Everything in existence in this universe is in constant vibration. There is hard science for this and no one should disagree, although you have the right to do so. The law of vibration is a law, just like the law of gravity. If you jump off a building, you will fall, regardless of your religious beliefs or your stubbornness. The same goes with the law of vibration. The law of vibration is the explanation that explains how everything in this world is energy, and you are one great source of energy. Everything within the universe consists energy. Even matter is energy as Einstein explained with his insight that E=mc2 (Energy is equal to Mass the Speed of light squared). His formula shows that matter and energy are actually the same thing and you can convert between the two which is what nuclear reactors and trees do when they use photosynthesis to eat. The law of vibration is the happy medium between quantum physics and new-age philosophers, which I am sure they will say that I am. However, I am so in love with Quantum Physics and have spent massive amounts of money learning the wacky things within it, I see myself as more of a quantum physicist than philosopher, but I do know how to marry the two better than most people.

Here is what we know in the quantum physics world:

Matter is mostly empty space with tiny wave-like particles (atoms and their sub-atomic building blocks) vibrating around each other. We know this to be factually, so there is no real reason to disagree here. Light is now explained through the wave/particle theory, there is a fantastic experiment called the *Double Slit Experiment* that will give you more insight to this, and sound is just vibration through a medium (e.g. air) too. Both light and sound is simply energy that is vibrating. Everything vibrates at different frequencies. Again, It is essential that you understand that everything within the universe vibrates before you can start using the Law of Vibration and you will simply attract to you what is vibrating at your frequency.

I attended a science seminar some time back and this was said,

Even something as solid as a rock is always vibrating at a certain frequency and we can see it through light vibrations or touch it or even perhaps smell it. This is because the rock consists of matter, and ultimately all matter consists of atoms.   The law of vibration states everything vibrates.   This includes what we see, hear, smell, touch, taste and the material our bodies are made

So Happy and Grateful

Antonio T.Smith, Jr

*of, right through to what we
think and feel.*

Essentially, everything is in vibration. We as human beings are essentially vibration sensors since all our senses are just allowing us to experience vibrations of different frequencies with our physical bodies. Our eyes see a blue sky because the blue rays of light move at a vibration slow enough for our retinas to process. We see colors but only the colors that vibrate at a frequency we can process. We hear sounds, but only the sounds that are at a frequency low enough for the vibration of our ear drums to translate into noise, music, or language.

Just because you cannot see, hear or detect that something vibrates at a certain frequency does not mean that it ' s not vibrating. For example, tectonic plates vibrate at a frequency at all times, then rub against one another. When they rub against another violently they create an earthquake. Meanwhile, the buildings in any city are vibrating at a frequency as well. Yet, when the frequency of the buildings match the frequency of the earthquakes, the buildings will collapse. Pay close attention here, because it is only the buildings that match the frequency of the earth quake that will fall. Most of you are matching the frequency of the destructive forces in this world. Therefore, you fall. There is so much more out there than you're aware of, but you've been so conditioned to believe that something is only real if you can perceive it with your physical body and senses. This is simply not true.

So Happy and Grateful

Antonio T.Smith, Jr

What is a belief? Belief is simply a thought that gains momentum. It is an idea that has gained tons of emotion over time, and it is beliefs that become manifestations. Your actions are not calling the shots. The law of attraction is not responding to your actions, it is responding to your beliefs. Your job is to find the belief that inspires your actions and then you can manifest the result you want. Yet, most people look at their actions and then work against themselves and create a belief to explain their actions. "Oh, I must be stupid because

I made a mistake. " This is monitoring the action and then developing the belief that you are stupid because you did an action that wasn' t necessarily smart. Your actions do not define you, as most people say. Your beliefs control your actions; therefore, your beliefs define you.

The Law of Attraction and The Law of Vibration

There is something called vibrational magnetism and the Law of Attraction works through this. If I were to say this more simply, I would say, *like attracts like*. Energy attracts its similar energy because the wave forms match one another. Let us examine energy and thoughts for one moment. If everything in this world is energy, then the greatest form of energy is thought. I want you to think about this for a second. Very few people will disagree with this, but I will address them nonetheless. Someone may say that the sun is the greatest form of energy in the universe because it gives life. This is a pretty sound argument, but to that I will say, "The sun isn't building skyscrapers, creating businesses, or enjoying smartphones or wifi. " Of course, this is written in a jokingly manner, but there is a lot of truth here. Human beings have done more with thought than any other species on the planet. Elephants aren't writing novels, birds are airplane mechanics, and birds were flying eons before humans were. Thought, my friend, is the highest form of energy. Now, back to the point. If everything in this world is energy, then the greatest form of energy is thought. For the most part, all activity within your brain is measured in waves. Different emotions

So Happy and Grateful

Antonio T.Smith, Jr

equal different waves and each wave will attract something of its kind. You can' t plant a banana and get back an orange. You must always get back what you planted in the same kindness. What you plant is what will come back to you and it will come back to you in great multiplication. The same goes with thoughts. You get back what you think, remember, I will go deeper into thoughts in the next chapter, but you will get a great multiplication of your thoughts. You are constantly emitting waves of different frequencies, and the types of waves you emit depends on

So Happy and Grateful

Antonio T.Smith, Jr

the thoughts you think and the emotions you have attached to those thoughts. Put that together with the fact that frequencies attract similar frequencies, and you will be left with the Law of Attraction. What you think about is what you attract like a magnet or like gravity. This is why if you think negative thoughts you will receive negative things and if you think positive thoughts you will receive positive things.

Here Is Where All of This Gets Spooky

The universe has limits that are unknown and you are a major part of the universe's power. It is true that you are a physical body, but you are so much more. Let us take for example, the Protagonist of the Christian Sacred Text, Jesus Christ. This is not a religious example, but a metaphysical example instead. Without believing in the belief system, but simply observing the narrative that was recorded. Jesus had amazing-manifesting-power while being in a physical body. This is you. You have more in common that Jesus than you actually think, when you simply observed the narrative. You have amazing-manifesting-power in your physical body and you can call forth anything you desire if you simply have faith. Unfortunately, many of you have not realized this potential because you are waiting for someone to guide you. There is no reason to wait for anyone to guide. Of course, there is nothing wrong with a guide or mentor, but no one can guide you accurately. There is not a mentor in the world, coach, religion, or school of thought that can guide you accurately, because you already have built-in guidance. Your feelings are your ultimately guide and all you need to do is train your autosuggestion to allow you to interpret your feelings correctly.

Napoleon Hill defines autosuggestion as:

The faculty of being able to concentrate your mind on your burning desire until your subconscious mind accepts it as

*fact and begins to devise ways
of bringing it about.*

Essentially, you can only do what you have trained your autosuggestion to do and you can only see what you have trained it to see. This is a feeling world but if you can't get your autosuggestion under control, then you will interpret your feeling incorrectly most of the time.

Here is how Napoleon Hill teaches you how to develop your autosuggestion, when it comes to money. I will touch on this much more in Chapter 27, but for now, we can discuss it here.

Napoleon Hill ' s Formula for Developing the Principal of Auto Suggestion – Source: *Think And Grow Rich*.

> 1. *Go into some quiet spot, perhaps in bed at night. Close your eyes and repeat aloud so you may hear your own words the written statement of the amount of money you intend to*

accumulate, the time limit for its accumulation, and a description of the service you intend to give in return for the money. As you carry out these instructions, see yourself already in possession of your goal.

By the first day of xxx, I will have in my possession $xxx which will come to me in various amounts from time to time during the interim.

So Happy and Grateful

Antonio T.Smith, Jr

In return for this money, I will give the most efficient service of which I am capable of rendering the fullest possible quantity, and the best possible quality of service in the capacity of xxx.

I believe that I will have this money in my possession. My faith is so strong that I can now see this money before my eyes. I can hold it in my hands. It is now awaiting transfer to me at the time and in the proportion that I deliver the

So Happy and Grateful

Antonio T.Smith, Jr

service I intend to render in return for it.

I have a plan by which to accumulate this money and I will follow that plan with a burning desire and unwavering persistence regardless of obstacles.

1. Repeat this program night and morning until you can see in your imagination the money you intend to accumulate.

So Happy and Grateful

Antonio T.Smith, Jr

2. Place a written copy of your statement where you can see it night and morning and read it just before retiring and upon arising until it's been memorized. These steps are auto suggestion.

What I would like to say here is mostly focused on number one of Formula for Developing the Principal of Auto Suggestion. When it comes to the law of attraction, all you have to do is be specific about what you want and when you want to experience it, and then see yourself in possession of it, because it already exist in the universe. You don' t have to earn it, you have already earned it, you simply have to call it into your existence. The important thing to remember here is that the money you want already existence and it is vibrating at a certain frequency, and all you have to do is speak what you desire loud and often enough until you convince yourself that it can happen, write it down so you can see it, be definite and specific about what you want so you can vibrate at its specific frequency, say when you want to experience to change your thoughts into beliefs, be willing to attract your desire by serving others, and see yourself with it so much that you can't tell the difference between having it and not having it. This is all you have to do. The law of Attraction does not discriminate. It will always allow you the freedom to choose.

Lessons From Fred Alan Wolf, Earl Nightingale, And Abraham Hicks

One of my favorite people lately has become Dr. Fred Alan Wold, quantum physicist. By now in this book, it is obvious that I enjoy a fact-based world, but I equally enjoy the invisible that cannot be seen so easily as what we perceive to be to be the face-based world. Dr Wolf has become a voice I enjoy to hear in the weirdness of life.

Let's take this quote for example:

(...) I try to explain to people that the basic of understanding

that we physicists have of how the universe works is not based upon the Law of Attraction. What it is based upon is that there seems to be the presence of something called Mind, or something outside of the physical world, which seems to be needed or present in order to explain, completely, the observations of reality that we have been able to carry out up to now. – Dr. Fred Alan Wolf

So Happy and Grateful

Antonio T.Smith, Jr

What Dr. Wolf is doing here is uplifting the power of the mind, or consciousness. He has once said, " Reality cannot exist without the mind entering into it. " Therefore, reality cannot exist without your mind, ladies and gentleman. Concurrently, your mind can only create a reality that your autosuggestion can handle, which means, the higher you awareness, the better your reality. If you acknowledge that the law of attraction is a major factor in the experience of your life, you will be more careful the next time you complain or dive deep into conversations that do not serve you.

Let's take another quote from Dr. Wolf

> "You may be thinking, "Well, that's very nice, but I can't do that." or "She won't let me do that!" or, "He'll never let me do that." or, "I haven't got enough money to do that." or, "I'm not strong enough to do that." or, "I'm not rich enough to do that." or "I'm not, I'm not, I'm not, I'm not." Every

single "I'm not" is a creation!"

Every I' m not is a creation. Truer words have never been spoken. Negative energy is so powerful that it takes three grades of 100 to make a zero average to a 75 in school. Think about this for a moment and let' s equate it to an "I' m not" or an I can' t". If for every one time you said I' m not or I can' t this year, you needed to beleive at 100% just to be average, how many 100% beliefs would you need to neutralize all the negative creations you have had this year. This completely explains why many people don't believe the law of attraction because they believe it does not work for them. Yet, it does. It has always worked. Your negative thoughts, whether you are conscious of them or unconscious of them are the thoughts you have created for most of your life.

We live today in a golden age but we do not take advantage of this age. Instead, we complain while our pockets contain all the access to the known and unknown world. Yet, we don't use what we can. Earl Nightingale defines success as, " The progressive realization of a worthy ideal. " I truly believe may be the best definition of success possible. He identifies that the pursuit of success will be progressive— as in ongoing, and that the target one is aiming for must be a worthy ideal *to them*. Therefore successful is individualize, but the pursuit of the ideal someone is aiming for must be with maximum effort. I love this.

I believe I have created the second best definition of success. it contains three parts. **For me, success is** anyone who sets a target, hits that target, and hits the target well. Through my experience, most people don't even have a target, which immediately eliminates them from being successful. If you have no target, you have no success. Secondly, you have to actually hit the target. In my experience, most people set a target and then they begin to fake a good harvest by buying things that make them look as if they have hit the target. They go through the motions of being successful but they are not actually successful. In the social media age, they post a successful life, but they have not actually hit the target. They have created images that suggest they have hit the target. Lastly, how you hit your target matters. If you use people to hit your target, hurt, and abuse people, then you are not successful. You have the fruit of success, but everyone eventually gets what they have planted into the ground, one way or another. True success does not need to be protected or defended. True success does not create lack for others, but opportunities for others to succeed. On the other end of the spectrum, if you happen to get what you want but you did it with a bad attitude, then your success is only limited due to the law of attraction, and in my opinion, limited success is not success. I will never limit my success or allow for you to do so, because the universe has no limits. Once you place a limit on success, it is no longer success. It becomes well dressed poverty, because limited success has lack in it, and there is no such thing as lack. This is a concept I will go deeper into in Chapter 27. What do you think of my definition of success? I

So Happy and Grateful

Antonio T.Smith, Jr

would love to hear about it. Share your thoughts with me on my Facebook page at fb.com/theatsjr. Every one of us is the sum total of his or her thoughts, whether you like this or not. You have been guided by your mind and your mind has determined your reality.

Life should be an exciting adventure, it should not be a bore. – Earl Nightingale

It would be disrespectful to teach this deeply on the law of attraction without bringing up Bob Proctor and Abraham Hicks, and since I have mention Bob

Proctor earlier in this chapter I will now summon Abraham Hicks. Here are her teachings on the law of attraction below:

1. You are a physical extension of that which is non-pyhsical.
2. You are here in this body because you chose to be here.
3. The basis of your life is freedom; The purpose of your life is joy.
4. You are a creator; you create with your every thought.

5. Anything that you can imagine is yours to be or do or have.

6. As you are choosing your thoughts, your emotions are guiding you.

7. The universe adores you for it knows your broadest intentions.

8. Relax into your natural well-being. All is well. (Really it is.)

9. You are a creator of thoughtways on your unique path of joy.

10. Actions to be taken and possessions to be exchanged are

by-products of your focus on joy.

11. You may appropriately depart your body without illness or pain.

12. You can not die; You are everlasting life.

We will end this section with one more quote from Dr. Fred Alan Wolf. It is perhaps my favorite quote of his.

" I want to tell you something. You're God in disguise. " -Fred Alan Wolf

So Happy and Grateful

Antonio T.Smith, Jr

This is so beautiful to me. I hope it is the same to you. If you disagree, that is perfectly fine as well. I have very few core beliefs. The reason I have very few is because I tend to be a free thinker and open to all people and experiences of life. However, I have one core belief that rules them all. It is, **There is only one of us in the room.** We are all connected and anything less than that is just false. In the beginning there was all there is and all there was, was all there was — and all there was, was good. Then; here is where so many people disagree, humans were created. Whether you believe in randomness and disorder, or God and great order, no one can deny that if you cut us all open, we will all look the same. With this being said, we all came from the creative source. Astrologists will say, "We are all made of star stuff." Since we all come from the creative source, then Dr. Wolf is correct, you are just God in disguise. In some religious circles it is said that, "We are made in His image." In addition, you can create anything from absolutely nothing. Sounds like God power to me.

So Happy and Grateful

Antonio T.Smith, Jr

The Law of Opposites

To conclude this message, let us call upon Neale Donald Walsch one more time. He once said,

> *"In the absence of that which you are not, that which you are is not."*
>
> *With this single sentence, given to me in the very first Conversations with God book published in 1995, I was introduced to the Law of Opposites.*

So Happy and Grateful

Antonio T.Smith, Jr

I didn' t understand what was meant by that sentence when I first saw it come off my pen and most people with whom I have shared this wisdom do not "get it" the first time they hear it. Let' s look at the statement again and delve into its meaning.

"In the absence of that which you are not, that which you are is not. "

This sentence is very powerful. For me it is one of THE most powerful and illuminating statements in all of the Conversations with God material - and that stretches across nine very important books.

The sentence means that we live in a world of relativity. Everything here is experienced relative to something else, and when there is no "something else," there is no ability to experience what is being experienced.

Before I explain what this means, it is important to understand that most people who attempt to use the law of attraction in their favor don't understand this law, so they feel the law of attraction doesn't work for them or isn't real. This is simply not true. The law of attraction has always worked for you, you just did not use it use it in a manner that served your dreams.

The understanding of the law of opposites was revealed to Neale during the process of writing his book that changed the world. The best way for me to explain this to all of you is to say

So Happy and Grateful

it this way. The moment you fix in your mind what you want, everything that is opposite of what you desire will be manifested into your life before you get what you desire. Fundamentally, when you want something, everything you don't want — that is in the opposite frequency of what you do want will come to you first and you *must* deal with it in order to enjoy what you desire. Think of it in another manner. If you desire a hot shower, the experience of being dirty must appear in your reality first, or you will not be able to enjoy the hot shower. If everyday of your life was only hot showers and nothing else, you would not enjoy the hot water pressing against your skin and washing you clean, because there would be no opposite to invoke the experience of enjoyment. If you can' t wait to go home and eat your favorite meal, you must first be away from home and eating something you must settle for, then you will be able to enjoy what you truly desire— which is to be home and to enjoy your favorite meal.

It the real world, ladies and gentleman, you *must* invoke the opposite of what you want **first** in order to enjoy what you are intentionally attracting. If you are attracting a lot of money, you must first experience the opposite of a lot of money for a season, so when you do get what you desire, you are able to enjoy it. You are a being, but in order to be one, you must first obtain knowledge, then move to experience, and only when you have a perfect harmony of both will you be able to master **being**. You are not here to skip over the experience part of life, no matter how much you would like. To get true love, you must first have your heart broken. To get health, you must first become sick. To get married, you must first be single. To drink water, you must first grow thirsty.

The reason the law of attraction isn't working for you is because when you invoke it, you quit when the opposites show up in your life, but that is how it all works. It is part of the law of attraction. It is what you need to get what you want. If you want it to work for you, stop quoting and stop letting the opposites of life alter your mood. The trick to mastering the law of opposites is to simply embrace what has come into your reality and stop fighting it. To fight is to resist, and disease is the law of attractions response to resistance. Simply relax in our body and embrace the fact that was has come into your reality is 100% under your control and you are always on your way to what you desire, even if you take a longer route than what was available.

So Happy and Grateful

Antonio T.Smith, Jr

Transformational Exercises

Define the Law of Vibration.

Define Law of Attraction.

Identify your target. Write it down here.

How will you hit this target? Write it down here.

Think about how you can use the LOA to service your dreams. Write those thoughts here.

So Happy and Grateful

Antonio T.Smith, Jr

From the thoughts above write 10 statements that begin this way: I am so happy and grateful now that...

Complete each statement by acknowledging receipt of something you want.

Repeat these statements every morning and evening adding more as you begin to vibrate at higher frequencies.

The Law of Deliberate Creation

THE REASON YOU AREN'T GETTING IT

Chapter 11

So Happy and Grateful

Antonio T.Smith, Jr

Breaking The Cycle of Repetitious Living

How do you break the cycle of repetitious living? This is a million dollar. How do you give more of you to yourself? Additionally, how do you give more to others without bankrupting yourself, because giving more money is not giving more of yourself. Many of us treat our symptoms but never treat our actually problem. Who among you, dear readers, feel tied up, stressed out, overworked and under appreciated. You have to break the cycle. Pain is not normal it is just a part of life.

This chapter will help you recognize the reason why you are trapped in a cycle of repetitious living. I will also offer you a solution. In fairness, I cannot take full credit for this chapter, or the next chapter. Simply because Esther (Abraham) Hicks teaches on this subject better than anyone on planet earth. Therefore, you may read some overlap from her ideas and my own, which is completely fair because she doesn't t leave too much meat left on the bones of this subject. Moreover, I will introduce some new thoughts in this chapter that may be helpful to you.

If you are in an abusive relationship, the abuse is not the problem, it is the symptom. If you don't active listen and it is hurting your business and income, that is not the problem, that is the symptom. The problem, dear reader, is you! You are the problem. All of your blessing flow through you. Likewise, all of your problems flow through you.

Most people in life are trapped, because in the absence of purpose they are only left to play games. Life is not a game, life is a big ball of events that resemble a game, but you must take life seriously because the only way you can get out the game is to die.

Let's talk about prayer for a moment. When attempting to use prayer to break the negative cycle in your life, it is more important to be less aware of where you are and more aware of more of who you are. When you are in a constant state of prayer, you are also in a constant state of *asking*. Yet, you don't have to ask for anything because you already have everything.

So Happy and Grateful

Antonio T.Smith, Jr

In the " Ask, Believe, Receive " formula, the ask isn' t necessary and asking vibration, but a declaration vibration. When you concentrate on where you are in your situation, you are reminded of what you do not have. When you concentrate on who you are in prayer, you are reminded of your unlimited power. Most people pray from a place of lack. Prayers should focus more on the appreciation of things. If you don' t have what you desire in this time in your life, you can appreciate the awareness of this moment and it will attract to you what you desire. If

So Happy and Grateful

Antonio T.Smith, Jr

you like yourself when you pray, source you will appreciate this vibration and move into motion what you have asked for and the great Creative Source will honor it and grant your request. Likewise, if you like where you are in your situation when you pray, source you will appreciate this vibration and move into motion what you have asked for and the great Creative Source will honor it and grant your request. A prayer that comes from the awareness of need is counter to your value. It is the antithesis to your actual desire. It is the poison that sabotages prayer.

So Happy and Grateful

Antonio T.Smith, Jr

Source Energy is always comfortable where it is. It is always happy with itself, and you are an extension of source energy. You can' t hate yourself but love your Creative Source and expect to get the fullness out of life. The goal is to be *in control of what is happening to you.* Ladies and gentleman, you control what happens to you. Make sure you reach the point of unconditionally appreciate and you will be able to begin to tackle the breaking the cycle of repetitious behavior. Conditional appreciate is the poison that keeps the gears of your negative cycle moving.

Struggle Is Not Necessary

Hard times give birth do desire. Since you all have the experience of this, I must tread lightly to get you to fully understand that struggle is not necessary. Struggling or having hard times is necessary to the whole of things, but it is not necessary to win and dominate your reality. In fact, struggle is a mediocre and slow way of moving forward. Your ultimate goal is to have the frequency of your being match the frequency of your desires. There is no real struggle when you do this. Sure, you may first experience the opposite of what you desire when you are vibrating at what you desire, but when you understand the law of opposites, the struggle is taken away. You cannot desire great things and think you are a little person.

If you enjoy the person of Jesus, in Luke 11:1-13 you will hear some of Jesus' thoughts are prayer. It is evident from Luke's Gospel that Jesus prays often (Luke 3:21; 5:16; 6:12;

9:18, 28). Jesus starts His instruction by saying , " When you pray. " For the follower of Christ, prayer is not a matter of if, but when. So, it is probably safe to say that at some point in your life you will pray, even if you don' t follow religion, you will do something that will put you in the category of prayer. Prayer or medication is designed to help you vibrate at the frequency of what you desired, they also help you find a place without struggle. When you get to the place in which you are not struggling, that is when you begin to deliberately create your reality. Let us see if we can simplify this into a better understanding and provide some practical steps for mastering deliberately creating your life. Prayer is not the action of struggle. Prayer is the action in which you leave struggle

The idea of struggling to get what you want is not a proper idea. The idea that one must struggle or strive, or to be uncomfortable just to achieve is going about success the wrong way. You are all genius creators that can manifest whatever you desire and struggle is not an essential ingredient to success.

The Law of Deliberate Creation

Up until this point, I have done a good job by not being complex, but I cannot avoid it now. We have reached the point in which I take us higher in order to make this understandable and practical for your benefit. When understanding the Law of Creation, man must know that he is part of Creation. All life forms and energies are part of the Creation. This means that you are not separate from creation nor are you disconnected from the Creator. You are part of the creation like your children are part of you, if you have kids. If not, then you are part of creation like you are part of your parents. There is no separation, just only an individual experience that creates the illusion of separation. Think about it this way. You are completed connected to your parents. You were gifted 100% of half of their chromosomes. Which basically gave you all the best of both of your parents. Should you forget that you are forever connected with your parents, your chromosomes will not. Should you consciously deny that you are connected to your parents, your chromosomes won' t let you forget. You are what you are and you are connected to what gave you life. In the same manner, the Creative Source gave you life and you are unlimited like the Creative Source and of the same substance— just like your parents. You are part of creation and you cannot put yourself above creation, but you are the master of creation— your own.

Essentially, man can' t put himself above Creation and most importantly,

So Happy and Grateful

Antonio T.Smith, Jr

man must know that all living things are part of the same Creation and share in the same energy. Therefore, we are all connected— every human and every creature. And we have a responsibility to create a world in which we can all thrive. Yet, the only way we can create this world is to take responsibility for creating a great world for ourselves. In truth, we are all master creators. We create our lives every moment of every day, but we do not do so deliberately. Most of us create by default instead of deliberation.

So Happy and Grateful

Antonio T.Smith, Jr

The confusion that most people will have about creating their own realities is this: The more people focus on "what is missing from my now" they are creating the abundance of lack in their now. It is not that life is not giving you want you want, on the contrary, life doesn't take things away from you, nor does nature create or produce lack. Nature only creates abundance. You are either getting and abundance of prosperity with every creation of your life or you are getting an abundance of poverty each creation of your life. Creating is

So Happy and Grateful

Antonio T.Smith, Jr

about identifying what you want and to stay in an "So Happy And Grateful" mood, in order for the thing you are desiring to manifest in your life. In short, if you let *now* bother you, you will not get the prize. Don't let your *now* mess up your life. Appreciate your *now* and you will begin to deliberately create your reality. Whatever you keep paying attention to in your reality is what is going to continue to repeating itself into your reality. If you want something that you do not yet have, don't pay attention to the lack of having this thing. Instead, pay attention to how it exist in your imagination and how it makes you feel when you when as you focus on that thing. As you create in your mind what you want, exceeding optimism about what you have created should be your very next step. The more you are happy about what you have created and the more you become happy about receiving your creation, the faster the universe will bring that into existence for you.

We are all master creators and you and I are now having a leading edge conversation. Yet, two of the worst things that could have ever happened to you was having access to adults and becoming an adult yourself. Had you read this book earlier in your life or had a conversation with me as a child, this information would not be so hard for you to accept. Think of children. Children don't have to be reminded to have fun and be optimistic about gifts that are coming. They look forward to holidays and live in a constant state of expectancy until some adult tells them, *"Money doesn't grow on trees.* Think about this for a second. The child is happy and in the proper state of expectancy and is calling the gift into existence, and the adult, usually a parent, knocks all the optimism out of them and plants realistic thoughts into their mind. Yet, poverty is not a realistic thought. Poverty is actually the insane thoughts of the greatness of our beings. Poverty is not holy and poverty is not normal. We have just normalized it. We have become okay with homeless people in the streets. We have also accepted that thousands of children dying from starvation every day, while established countries waste more food per day than is needed to feed those children. All of this is poverty.

So Happy and Grateful

Antonio T.Smith, Jr

To knock optimism out of a child, which breaks the attraction process, is the definition of poverty. It is not normal to leave poor and without, we have just normalized it in society.

When you are desiring the same dream, you tend to ask the same question over and over. When you want your problem solved, you are constantly asking questions to get the problem solved. "How can I do this? "What is is going to take for this to go away? " The more you focus on the question and the problem is the more you keep yourself away form the solution. Think about this for a second. The universe is far smarter than you. If you are religious, your God is far smarter than you. With this understanding, why do you think you have to keep repeating the question. Your next best move in this scenario is to put distance between the problem/question and the solution/answer. You can only do this with happiness. It is happiness that will daw that to you. I am not taking practicality out of the equation. Believe me, I am on the most practical people alive. I am simply suggesting that having all your focus on the problem is counterproductive to you're receiving the solution. Once you know exactly what you want, forget about the wanting and the move into the complete joy of receiving what you once wanted. The answer has already been answered for you. The reason you are not receiving the answer is because you are too wrapped up in the question. If you never allow the solution to enter your life, you will always be entangled with the problem you want to disappear— more on this in the next chapter.

So Happy and Grateful

Antonio T.Smith, Jr

You are currently creating your reality right now and you have always had this power. It is what you will do five minutes from now, and it is what you will do 5 hours from now. You are always receiving what you are wanting, even if you not aware of what you want or not willing to admit you wanted something that is not currently serving you. All things in your life have been invited by you, even if you do not want it. You are the conscious observer. You are the magnet to your desire. What you and I must now do is get you to understand why you are getting what you are getting, because more than likely, you have attracted things into your life that are not worthy of you. Let's change this together.

Some Things To Remember

There are a few things that I want you to remember:

1. The Universe cannot stop delivering to you. You are always receiving from the universe at every second of every day.

2. You cannot control your blessings, you can only manifest them. Any attempt to control how the things you desire come to you, will simply cancel them coming to you.

3. Have a specific and definite plant for what you desire. Napoleon Hill was the first to popularize this notion, I am simply reiterating it. The universe is an ordered-being. It is not confused. Whatever your dominate thoughts and

frequencies are, that is what you will receive.

4. Write down what you want and read it aloud twice daily. This is another jewel from Napoleon Hill's *Think And Grow Rich*, but it is worth mentioning. To read aloud what you want before you go to bed and before you begin your day, is to also reprogram your subconscious to agree with your dreams and desires. You cannot get anything consciously speaking of a thing, but subconsciously repelling it.

So Happy and Grateful

Antonio T.Smith, Jr

5. Find yourself in a state of happiness to where people love to be around you. Only through happiness can you complete the steps of *Believe and Receive*, which are the blue prints to completing a manifestation of what you desire.

6. You have to have it before you can have it. This can be a hard concept to grasp, but it is actually quite simple. In order to receive a thing you desire, you must already act as if you have it in your hands or in your

reality. The stronger that feeling gets, the more you are sure to manifest what you desire.

7. Make sure your actions match what you desire. You can't desire to lose weight and still eat things that make you gain wait. You can't have both your desire and your poison and expect to manifest your breakthrough.

8. See the good in everything. Life is not bad and nothing is happening to you, it is all

happening for you. The faster you can wrap your mind around that, is the faster you can wrap your hands around your manifestations.

Stop Canceling What You Want

These are my final words in this chapter. Stop saying phrases like, *"But it is too expensive."* *If it is in God's will."* , *and the one that hurt me the most,* *"I need."*Let's talk about all three of these.

But it is too expensive. There have been many dreams that have been killed this way. " I would like to go to college, **But it is too expensive.** " The moment you said that you would like to go to college, that creation was on the way to you. And then you did it. You canceled it. You brought in your realistic mind and said *but.* Don' t do this again. Instead, say, "I want to go to college, **how can I acquire the money to do so.** This sentence structure comes with a fantastic vibration, keeps your mind open to receiving what is good about this world, and leads to the manifestation of you obtaining your college degree.

If it is in God's will. I will tread lightly here. Not because I am wrong, rather because religion is tied to into the strongest of emotions and emotions are central to the creative process. There is absolutely no difference between saying, *"If it is in God's will."* or *"but I can't afford it."* These two phrases carry the same negative emotion— even if you have mad that negative emotion holy. God has already given you permission to be in abundance, you do not have to ask your

God if abundance is something you can experience. Abundance is your birthright and you do not have to beg for what is already yours.

I need. Dear Reader, this one has been the toughest for me. I said, "I need" for so long that it became the natural way that I communicate. I find it funny that I had to teach myself how to do poverty things. When you come from a place of *I need* you are admitting that you do not have. The moment that you admit what you do not have something, you separate yourself from every possible future version of you who has everything you have ever created for yourself. Do yourself a favor and never try to manifest anything of prosperity from a position of lack. You will only frustrate yourself and doom yourself to more poverty.

The Thing You Have Been Missing

There is a vibrational version of everything before that thing can exist in your reality. If I had to say this another way, I would say, "You have manifestation all wrong. Why have you convinced yourself that when you see something that is the moment you have manifested it. No! This is all wrong. The vibration of that manifestation existed first, and then you pulled it into your physical reality. Yet, when you do not understand this, you are not a creator, but a reactor. You live your life but what you have observed. Therefore, you keep yourself in the same cycle of unhappiness, because you only react to what you have seen. The thing you have been missing here is simple: *It is not what you have seen that makes you feel sad or angry,*

So Happy and Grateful

Antonio T.Smith, Jr

actually, it is you always feeling sad or angry that brings about what you have seen.

You basically want life to give you something better so you can have a better response to it. Again, this is all wrong. You have to have the better response first and then the better life you wish to experience will follow. This is the truth and will continue to be the truth. Each and ever time. Do yourself a favor and realize that what is happening outside of you doesn' t mean anything, but what is happening within you means everything.

So Happy and Grateful

Antonio T.Smith, Jr

I Have A Friend Who Should Know Better

I have a friend who has a high level of awareness but a very low level of forgiveness. Let's call her Carla. Carla is kind to everyone because Carla knows the actually truth. Carla knows she is a very mean person. She only cares about herself and the one family member she loves. Of course, Carla will tell you that she loves everyone in her family, but deep down, she knows she only has time for one and gives energy to one. It would be nice if Carla would accept this true reality of herself, her harvest proves it day in and day out. However, Carla has a reputation of being kind and gentle because she is quiet and she has allowed herself to believe her reputation. Yet, her reputation is only a harvest of her ability to keep people away from her. She doesn't let anyone in and as of this writing, has no immediate plans to do so. Carla is doing herself a major disservice because Carla won't pay attention to her actual harvest. Should Carla pay attention, she would see that her harvest financially hurts the family member she love, and

So Happy and Grateful

Antonio T.Smith, Jr

financially hurts the people who are trying to love her. Of course, finances aren' t everything, but they are most certainly the most important thing to Carla and in this season of her life she needs money now more than ever.

Yet, money doesn' t love Carla. It can' t. Carla is a very mean person so money is very mean to her. Carla has not figured out her relationship with herself, because she is so busy not letting people get close enough to her that she never has enough energy to get close to herself. Moreover, when Carla does take the time to draw closer to herself, Carla mostly goes within mediation to prove people wrong so she can be right. This is Carla ladies and gentleman. She has very little working well in her life because she works very little to make others lives well. You will always create into your reality what you are, not what you want. And, until you align what you are with what you want, you will continue to be just like Carla. Odds are, you are Carla. Your details are just a tad bit different.

Let's end this chapter with Carla. When you soften resistance, you can begin to create your own reality after your own liking. However, as long as you are not genuine with people, especially the people you love, you will never be happy and you will never deliberately get what you want.

Transformational Exercises

Write down your plan to get out of your cycle of living and to break into the one that serves you. Write down what you intend to be next year, how much money you plan to have, and how many major goals you plan to accomplish and make a plan for each of those major goals.

So Happy and Grateful

Antonio T.Smith, Jr

The Law of Allowing

UNDERSTANDING FREEDOM

Chapter 12

Stop Looking Through Beliefs That Blind You

So Happy and Grateful

Antonio T.Smith, Jr

Frustration is a clever way of *not* admitting that other people control your life. Whenever you are frustrated, you are now allowing what you desire to occur your life. Instead, you are tolerant or patient with circumstances you do not want to deal with in your life. To allow is to be at peace with yourself and to vibrate at the frequency of what you desire. To be tolerant or patient is to admit that you don' t like something in your life but have accepted it the fact that you are going to be ill-affected by it.

So Happy and Grateful

Antonio T.Smith, Jr

Pay attention to what frustrates you and come to the understanding that what frustrates you also controls you. In fact, what frustrates you most certainly keeps you away from what will make you happy.

Therefore, you must learn to create around you the world that you are wanting and allow others to create the world they want around them. Your world is your world and their world is their world. It is not enough to understand this intellectually but still have an issue with the way people choose to live. What they have chosen is what they have perceived to be what they deserve— even if they want to admit this or not.

Abraham Hicks would introduce this subject to you this way:

> *You are physical beings focused in a physical world, and you have accessed to much broader knowledge than most of you are allowing.* – *Abraham Hicks*

Basically, the Law of Allow is defined as you are a master creator constantly creating a reality that is perfectly in alignment with all that inside of you.

So Happy and Grateful

Antonio T.Smith, Jr

Likewise, others are master creators constantly creating a realities that are perfectly in alignment with all that inside of them. Therefore, there is never a reason to be in competition with anyone and to be bothered by whatever anyone else creates, because they have created what is perfect for them and you have likewise created what is perfect for you. Should you desire a different outcome, all you have to do is created — it is not the other person's job to create that reality for you.

So Happy and Grateful

Antonio T.Smith, Jr

Remember, you are born to be a creator because you are made of the Creator and share in the life of the Creator. The Creative Source of this world is so kind to you, it allows you to create whatever reality you choose without hindering your ability to do so. Likewise, you should do the same with other humans. They have the right to create the reality they desire, just the same as you.

So, let me repeat the them of this chapter. Stop looking though beliefs that blind you. You have so many other people' s thoughts in your head at this point in your life that you don't even know what you actually believe. You respond far more than you create. If you would decide right now that you don't need to wait for something good to happy, you will change your life and gain complete control over your happiness.

Let's Take A Flight

I want you to think about taking a flight and being in between your now and your dreams. Of course, we all know this is one of the most frustrating places to exist. We all know the "nows" of our lives aren' t always the most motivating moments in the world. In fact, sometimes, *now* can knock the life right out of you. Yet, now is all we have. With regards to time, *now* is all there ever is and will be. So, let' s take that flight. Can you see yourself. Protected by the aluminum of the plane and the pressurized cabin. You are 30, 000 feet in the air and all of a sudden, you get upset with the flight. You become frustrated in that the flight is never fair to you and you never got a chance to take a better

So Happy and Grateful

Antonio T.Smith, Jr

flight like other people. You become embarrassed by the location of your seats and you decide to run to the plan door, open it, and jump out the plane at 300,000 feet, while moving 400 miles per hour. That is what you would do, right? Of course not. Not only would you kill yourself, but anyone riding the plan with you will be killed. So my question to you is this: Why do you keep flying towards your dreams and then getting frustrated and fearful and then jumping out the plane to start all over again. Every time you jump out this dream-plane, you kill yourself and the people around you, only to start all over again. Here is a word of advice that I give to my team: Stay in the plan!

Stay in the plane my friend. Remember, Carla from the last chapter? She has hope. In fact, she has more hope than most. Carla was once a plane-jumper, but now Carla struggles inside that plane. She still can' t handle correction just yet, but one day she will. Why? She doesn' t leave the plane anymore. She is a fighter and she is learning to ONLY fight for prosperity. Therefore, however you felt about Carla in the last chapter, please know she will get to all she wants in life faster than most people in this world because she stays in the plane. I didn' t mention this in the last chapter because I wanted to highlight what was more important — that is to allow yourself to stay in the plane. Let' s go deeper.

The Many Things I Want To Share With You About Allowing

I' m sure there can be a library of books written about to the powerful things said by Abraham. For now let's focus on this one.

"Patience means to be tolerant about the not receiving mode."

Patience is not the same as trust but trust is the same as allowing. When you are patient about something, you are only tolerating your current reality and you will manifest more things to tolerate. My prayer for you is that this book will unlock something in your mind and teaches you to know that whatever you want is coming and all you need to do is allow it. Don't be patient about it not having arrived. Patience is not a positive emotion, it is putting up with something that doesn' t feel good. This is is a feeling that is working in the wrong direction for your happiness and your dreams.

When you feel regret you are not in receiving mode. Regret is the exact opposite of what you should be doing and regret and happiness does not live on the same road. So, don' t live in regret. If you haven' t not forgiven yourself for things you have done in your past, let it go for happiness sakes. If you are with someone who

So Happy and Grateful

Antonio T.Smith, Jr

refuses to forgive you for what you have done in your past, then let them go. Your happiness is vital to you living your best life.

Also, do not become realistic for this vibration holds what you want away from you. Realism is a bill of over-sold goods. Being realistic is the fastest way to poverty and the most subtle way to unhappiness. There is a beautiful world that you have never seen. It is the world that will serve you more than you could ever serve yourself— and you have never seen it in the real world of things. Yet, when you see it

in your mind' s world first, and allow this world to exist in your vibration, then this mind ' s wold becomes your real world. You see, the only way to manifest the beautiful things of this world is for you to NOT be realistic. You literally have to out-of-body experiences to enjoy this life in your body.

You only need one mindset to succeed in this world. That mindset is this: "I can' t see it yet but I trust that it is on the way. " This is the mindset that all of the great teachers before us have called *faith*.

Do your best to not become uncomfortable with the thought that you can turn thoughts into reality. You have been doing it since you were a baby when you learned that if you cried your parents would give you attention or food. You thought of the reality of their presence and with once action, you controlled free-willed adults as an infant. That is pretty impressive. Turning thoughts to things is what you are programmed to do. You are far better at this than you would ever think.

I also want to tell you that you are the maker of your own life. Everything, up to this point of your life, has been created by you. If you want something different, you don't have to uncreated things, you simply need to create what you do want and the experience of having what you do not want will no longer exist because you have all that you want.

Here is another thing, and probably the most important thing that I want to tell you in this chapter. Your job is

So Happy and Grateful

to get and receive glory and don't let anyone tell you anything different. If you can learn how to get and receive glory without looking down on others, then you would have truly mastered your life. Get what is yours because there is no such thing as lack and you get to have whatever you desire because you are a master creator. Don't worry about if others get what they desire, because they are also master creators and they can do the same. Remember, the happier you are, the better things will get.

Abundance has a vibrational frequency. You can tune into this

So Happy and Grateful

Antonio T.Smith, Jr

frequency with your feelings. Imagine for a moment what abundance feels like. Abundance is to never end, to never be short of, to have more than what you need. Think about what this actually means and how it actually feels. Can you remember a time when you had so much, you didn't mind helping others and giving a bit away? How did you feel when you did this? Giving some of your "enough" away probably didn't feel bad at all. That is because reality allowed you to feel abundance and abundance never minds giving. You should always walk around with this

So Happy and Grateful

Antonio T.Smith, Jr

feeling and you will be, do, or have anything that you want, because abundance attracts more abundance. Make a list of whatever you want and then ask yourself "what does having this feel like?" Once you have this feeling figured out, then the only thing you need to do is *allow* that feeling to take you over every day.

A bit of news that you would call bad. Until you have mastered the law of attraction and the law of deliberate creation, you cannot use the law of allowing. I am sorry, but this is just how it works. It is why I could not write a book about happiness and then leave these three laws out of it. They aren' t just part of the universal laws of happiness, they are essential laws to the laws of everything. When you have mastered the Law of Attraction and The Law of Deliberate Creation, then you will be able to truly say, "I am that I am and I am willing to allow others to be what they are." This is something Abraham Hicks says and to be honest, there is no one on earth that has ever said it better. When you master all three of these laws, you will let others be what they are without feeling bad for it. When you get to this point, then and only then will you experience true freedom. One who is tolerating their reality feels negative emotions, while one who is allowing feels the absence of negative emotion. The one who allows experiences freedom because you cannot have freedom with negative emotions. There is great value to giving attention to only the things that are important to you and to the things that serve you.

So Happy and Grateful

Antonio T.Smith, Jr

Don't Let Others Make You Feel Bad For Winning

Don' t lose sleep over being blessed when you worked your butt off to get it. It was you who decided to go to the gym while your friends were smoking weed. It was you who decided to eat healthy while your friends ate whatever they wanted to eat. Now, they want you to feel bad because they can' t bear the guilt of their own decisions. There is absolutely no reason for you to ever feel guilty for doing well in life. If you are blessed and you worked for everything you have, you have zero reasons to feel guilty for doing better than the people around you. Some people will never do anything with their lives and their time, and then expect you to do just as bad as them because they are uncomfortable with you doing well. Your job is to take care of your dreams!

Here are 5 reasons why you don't owe anyone an apology for doing well in life:

Winners Connect With Other Winners

If you are around people who are upset with you because you spend more time with your new friends than you spend with them, I want you to be very conscious of why you have made this change. Winners connect with winners and you realized that you can't win around the people you grew up with. Yes, they are family, but the family will rarely get you to the next level of your life. The family is more likely to keep the negative opinions of you because family rarely wants to be the lesser of the relatives. You found you a new family, some new friends, and you do not have to apologize for this! You aren't trying to replace anyone in your life, you are simply trying to be someone special in your own life.

People Talk Behind Your Back Because You Surpassed Them

The people who are talking behind your back can't handle that you have passed them up in life, as they see it, so they can't verbalize a "congratulations"; therefore, you only get the hatred that is always easier to manifest. When they talk about you, your only response should be humble winning. There is never a reason to argue with anyone who doesn't exist in your winning formula.

So Happy and Grateful

Antonio T.Smith, Jr

If they haven't contributed to your winning methods, politely ignore them and win some more, because winning is the only way to change their perception. Always remember, 50% of the NBA hated Kobe Bryant until his last game of his 20th season— Kobe scored 60 in his last game! That is how you treat people against. Don't argue, score!

You Don't Owe Anyone Anything

You don't owe them jack! This is your life and you don't have to live it for the approval of others. Most certainly, you should be living your life to add value to others, but you do not have to receive your value from others. The latter is detrimental to your health and self-esteem. Since you don't owe anyone anything, your value isn't determined by what they think of you. You deserve your blessings and you don't have to explain why you enjoy them so much to anyone!

You Don't Have To Live An Apology

One of the worst things I see in this world is good people who are forced to perform at a lower level because the people they love are expecting them to perform at a lower level. Why? Because they are still hurt by something you did to them years ago, and as long as you are around them, you aren't supposed to be doing well, because of what you did in the past.

Don't let people do that to you! So what you got pregnant before these people wanted you to. You've given birth, you take care of your child, and you deserve your dreams. So, what is the problem? Just because they have a low opinion of you doesn't mean you have to live up to it. Never, ever allow anyone to make you feel bad for being so blessed. Feed your kids, feed your family, be there for the people who need you most, but don't t pay their bills because you feel bad for doing so well. Everyone has to be responsible for them. Help them as much as you can, recognize people don't t start in the same places in life or with the same advantages, do what you can to help them, but never feel bad about the harvest you have earned!

So Happy and Grateful

Antonio T.Smith, Jr

The Reason They Have A Problem With Your Life Is Because They Don't Have One They Enjoy

They hate your life because they have created the life they want for themselves. Excuses sound best to the person making them up and they have millions of excuses for why they aren't winning and why you should feel bad for winning around them.

You can only control your harvest and influence the harvest of others.

When you get the two confused you will suffer. When you try to influence your own harvest and control the harvest of others, you don' t do enough work in your garden, and you spend too much time planting seeds in someone else' s with your energy and income, while they sit back and reap from your life source.

You have a choice. No one should feel bad for winning, especially you.

So Happy and Grateful

Antonio T.Smith, Jr

Transformational Exercises

Think about a situation or a person you have not yet released into this universe because they have hurt you. Decide at this moment that you completely forgive them and you no longer wish harm to them or to yourself. Picture them in your mind, say their name out loud and declare softly that you release them to be a master creator and you accept that you are a master creator. Before you move to the next chapter, completely let them or the situation go.

So Happy and Grateful

Antonio T.Smith, Jr

One Last Thing

BELIEVE

Chapter 13

I want to end this book with what you believe. Belief is an essential thing. Belief has everything to do with your philosophy. Whatever you can do in this life, please don't do it without believing.

So Happy and Grateful

Antonio T.Smith, Jr

When you know who you are, you also know who you are not. When you know who you are, you will never let anyone put something on you that does not fit.

You Can Do All Things

This is something you have to accept right now, without exception! The circumstances that you are in right now does not define your destiny. I am not talking about what you say; I am talking about what you believe about yourself. You know how to say all the right things, but you have to learn how to think all the right things. If you feel you are unlovable, you will be. If you feel you are dumb, you will be. People will do whatever it takes to make sure you are lower than them. Don't t worry about them and stop giving them energy! All you have to do is change your belief.

You are not too old to win, nor are you too old. You are just right. You are the perfect person. You are source unlimited. Stop being a person who wants people to like what you don't like and don't allow your past to bleed into your future.

So Happy and Grateful

Antonio T.Smith, Jr

Don't let life knock all the life out of you. You can't make good decisions from a bitter heart. Don't be bitter. Be happy. They will talk about you. Make sure they talk about you as you are on your way to the bank. They will talk badly about you, make sure they speak to you while you are having the time of your life. You belong to a place of prosperity. You may be going through hell right now, but hell has nothing on you because you are source unlimited.

All of us are survivors, or we wouldn't be here. We have survived the fire and the rain. We have survived divorce and unfaithfulness. This is your time. This is your moment! This is your life, and you are the only one who deserves to live it, so live! When you get ready to be happy, no one will be able to stop you. People will be upset when you get your blessing outside of them, but don't worry about that. Love them anyhow, because you are too happy to hate them.

Most people will make a withdrawal from your life when they don't benefit from it— make sure you never withdraw from you. *So Happy And Grateful* is a book about teaching people how to do more with their lives because some things in your life will make you run. I want to show you how to run after your destiny and not run from your fears. You have never seen a happy person running from joy. They only move towards happiness.

From Me To You

I know you can do anything and I am grateful you have bought this book. In truth, I could never repay you, so I will only tell you this. You are not what they say you are, even if they mean you are amazing. You are much more amazing than anything that I could ever describe. So, make sure you always watch what is growing up in your heart. Guard your happiness with everything you have in you.

When you change the direction of your happiness, you will modify the course of your living. Are you willing to be happy, regardless of who doesn't like it? Are you ready to demand out of life what is worthy of you? Anything you can focus your mind on, you can change. You don' t have to be anything you don' t want to be. The battleground between what you want and what you don' t want is happening in your mind. There is nothing in this life that is better than you and I will never stop you from believing this. If you don' t like the way your life is going, you are the only one that can change it. This is all about you, and this book has been all about you! There is nothing as powerful as a changed mind. So, where do you go from here? You go to self-actualization. What separates you from them is transformation.

So Happy and Grateful

Antonio T.Smith, Jr

So, I leave you with this. We are all going through a change. You don't have to be ashamed of yours. Let this be the year that you live the highest expression of yourself. I believe in you so much. I don't think anyone can write a self-help book and not believe in you. I have given you everything that I have within me. This is not my longest book, but it is my most intimate book on this subject. Whatever I am, you now have. Please use it, multiply it, and then do the same for someone else as you move forward.

So Happy and Grateful

Antonio T.Smith, Jr

Your Happiness Is Your Guide

What would you do if you knew that you can get past anything if you used your happiness? Your happiness is the road that is guiding you to the fulfillment of your wildest dreams. It allows you to tap into that part of you that will let you do more and be more. The greatest journey you can ever take is the journey of self-discovery, very few people continue this journey without being happy.

Yesterday doesn't matter as much as you think it does. Yesterday is only a reminder of either how stronger you have been, or should be. If you are wondering if now is the time where you go after your dreams and after your goals, the answer is yes! You know have to wait until you find out more, do more, or be more, because your time is now. When you tap into happiness, you can dream forward and plan backward. Success happens one step at a time. Dr. Topher Morrison says,

Inaction is still an action, it is just not an action that serves you.

So Happy and Grateful

Antonio T.Smith, Jr

I couldn' t agree more. This moment is precious. I understand how you can be afraid, but best life has already arrived. There is nothing you can do to stop it from coming, but you can do almost anything to make sure you don' t ride along with it.

Happiness is your foundation to a healthy life, but you can' t have the foundation of happiness around people with massive holes in theirs. I want you to take your life back. Sometimes taking back your life means to take away your presence from people who are not serving your happiness or your dreams. It is vital that you know exactly who you are because when you understand who you are, you will understand who shouldn't be in your life. One of the biggest mistakes that people make is thinking that happiness is easy. It is not easy, but it is your birthright. Happiness allows you to become the kind of person you wish to be before you become that person in reality.

So Happy and Grateful

Antonio T.Smith, Jr

Be Careful In Your Home

Home is the place where all you wish to acquire will be manifested or murdered. Your surroundings effect every single thing that you desire to be. If you have constantly trouble in your home, you will also have constant in your dreams. The entire universe is your playground, and this whole world is yours.

Life is far too short to argue all the time about everything. You were meant to do more than that, and so is your significant other. Clarity of thought and clarity of your vision is essential to your dreams, but you can' t reach the clarity you need when your home is killing your happiness.

Be A Pilot, Not A Passenger

Les Brown Says

> *If you are not willing to risk you can grow, and if you can' t grow, you cannot become your best. And if you cannot become your best, you can' t be happy — and if you can' t be happy then what else is there?*

He is right to ask, *what else is there*?
Can you think of something you have
done that changed your world or the
world of others, without being happy?
Sometimes your creation can lead to
your confusion. Your families can
confuse you. People's responses to
your sexual preference can confuse you.
Yet, you do not have to be confused,
because the only goal you should have
in life is to be happy. When you are
happy, you will move forward, and when
you forward, anything you need to
change will show up and add value unto
you.

So Happy and Grateful

Antonio T.Smith, Jr

Life is about being happy, even in unhappy times. You cannot control the world around you, what you can control are your thoughts. Your life and your legacy are in your hands. There will be things that happen to you that you cannot control. Stop responding to outside circumstances. There are no outside circumstances that can ever have power over you. You are the god of choice. So, stop making decisions in haste, because that is not the response of a god. When you learn to control your emotions and tap into your happiness,

So Happy and Grateful

Antonio T.Smith, Jr

you will make decisions from a higher place of awareness.

Start seeing your challenges as part of your quests. Winners hold their visions, even when they don't see any tangible results. When you continue to move forward, things will continue to appear for you. Always move forward, especially on the hard days. That is where winning lives— on the hard days. The hard days of life will always hold your life-changing breakthroughs.

Another thing about being a pilot is to know that you are making a difference in someone's life. Don't let people make you feel insignificant. You may be going through a divorce, but you are not insignificant. You may be a teenager mother, or have been a teenage mother, but you are not insignificant. You are not alone, and your life has value! You are important, and you are making a difference in someone's else's life. When you remember that you are making a difference, even to one person, you will find yourself in a state of gratitude. When you get to that place, you will be unstoppable, because there

So Happy and Grateful

Antonio T.Smith, Jr

is no force alive that has ever stopped genuine appreciation.

Honestly, if you are on the wrong road, get off it. It doesn' t serve you and stop trying to get to the end of it to see if it will eventually work out for you. The wrong road is not worthy of you. When you find out you are on the wrong path, turn.

Stop for one moment. If you are looking for approval from outside sources, you will never be happy. People will never validate you the way you need them to, only you can do that. Be grateful for your family, even if

So Happy and Grateful

Antonio T.Smith, Jr

they don't support you adequately. Don't worry about their level of support, make sure you live the life you were born to live.

You become what you think about, most of the time. You also become what you say to yourself, most of the time. When you master happiness, both of what you think about and what you say to yourself will be used to your advantage. To actually go through your entire life, only to discovered that you have never lived it will not be worthy of you.

Get up and live, because you get one shot at this world and that is it! I

So Happy and Grateful

Antonio T.Smith, Jr

encourage you to get in tune with yourself. Success is a process. Be patient and know that your time is coming. You cannot fail because failure doesn' t exist. Create your own trail where a path needs to be created. Every moment you spend outside of yourself looking for an answer to be happy is every minute you are not looking within to master your happiness.

Follow your happiness, don' t think about it. Do it. Listen to that still, soft voice. When you listen to this, there is some great power that none of us fully understand that will guide you to where you can achieve maximum happiness. This universe is alive. Get into the flow of it. You are special.

I will leave you with this next statement from my mentor Les Brown. He will say this better to you than I ever can.

If you want a thing bad enough
to go out and fight for it,
*   to work day and night for it,*
to give up your time, your peace

So Happy and Grateful

Antonio T.Smith, Jr

and sleep for it⋯ if all
that you dream and scheme is
about it,

⋯and life seems useless
and worthless without it⋯ if
you gladly

sweat for it and fret for it
and plan for it and lose all
your terror,

of the opposition for it⋯
if you simply go after that
thing that you

want with all your capacity,
strength and sagacity, faith
hope and confidence and stern

So Happy and Grateful

Antonio T.Smith, Jr

pertinacity···if neither cold, poverty, famine, nor gout, sickness nor pain, of body and brain, can keep you away from the thing that you want ··· if dogged and grim you beseech and beset it, with the help of God, YOU WILL GET IT! - Les Brown

If Things Aren't Working Out For You Right Now

Get your values in line with your dreams as fast as you can. Your values are a guide for you. They are your internal compass. When your values are not in line with your dreams, you can' t fulfill them. The trash you have to deal with on the way to your dreams doesn' t bother you as much when your values are in line with your dreams. You have to be obsessed with improvement and obsession will be the key to you applying the principles in this book.

Don' t be a slave to poverty another second. Don' t force other people to support your dreams when you don' t even support your own. You have to support you before you require others to support you. You have to love you before anyone else can love you properly. If you are down on your luck right now, get back up right now! Knocked down is a great place to be because it will remind you exactly where you do not want to be.

If you are not where you want to be it is because you are not who you are supposed to be. You are where you are because of who you are and if you want to be any where else you are going to have to change. If you don't move mountains for yourself no one will move mountains for you. Don't wait for something outside of you to rescue you.

So Happy and Grateful

Antonio T.Smith, Jr

You are your rescue and you don't need anything but that understanding.

How hungry are you! I remember being homeless. I remember sleeping in that trash can. I remember being raped and being molested, and because I remember it, I use it as motivation to never go back to any of those situations again. No one knows what Antonio T. Smith, Jr., is capable of but me. I know what I am capable of because I make it up every single day. I have no limits and I refuse to be limited. How about you? How do you feel

So Happy and Grateful

Antonio T.Smith, Jr

about your future? How do you feel
about your limitations?

Never Stop Moving Forward

If anyone has ever doubted you —
release them. Your dream will become a
reality as long as you stay happy and
stay focused. Sight is for people who
live in the present, all you need is
vision. Vision allows you to see in the
invisible world and pull things into
the visible world. You will not be a
failure because the only way to do that
is to quit and you will not quit.

So Happy and Grateful

Antonio T.Smith, Jr

I don't know who you are but I promise you that I gave everything I had to write this book. Write now, I am tired, my neck hurts, I'm tired of sitting in this chair, but I cannot stop because I can feel you. I can't explain it, but I can feel you. I can't stop writing because you and I both know that you are not living up to your potential and it is not killing you, but it is killing me. Step and live your dreams. Forget about what they called you when you were growing up. Take a step forward and live your dreams. Make up your mind and win. Everyone goes

So Happy and Grateful

Antonio T.Smith, Jr

through challenges, but everyone does not keep moving forward.

It is perfectly fine to keep moving forward. Here is some insight on how to do so:

- Stop apologizing for the good things in your life.
- If you pursue happiness, money will always find you; if you only pursue money and compromise happiness, money will never find you.
- You don't have to spend another day being sad

- The only people in your life who don't want you to win are the people who want to win more than you, but at the expense of your relationship with them.

- If you put a seed in the ground that serves you and it comes out the ground during harvest time, you don't have to apologize for putting in the work other people would not.

1. Winners connect with other winners.

So Happy and Grateful

Antonio T.Smith, Jr

- Winners hang with other winners so they can keep winning.
- Losers get together to talk about winners.
- Monitor your circle; you are who you hang around.
- Winners are trying to get all the abundance they can and share it.
- Winners do not co-mingle with sad people.
- Winners protect their gardens and don't let other people put bad seeds in them.
- Winners go where other winners go and read what other winners read.

So Happy and Grateful

Antonio T.Smith, Jr

- Winners do winner things.
- You're not much of a winner if you're not creating other winners.
- You can be a winner in a losing situation; losing does not make you a loser; having the mindset of a loser makes you a loser.

1. People talk behind your back as a winner because you have surpassed them.

- They are going to talk about you; make sure they talk about you winning.

- The more you rise in greatness is the more opportunity you create for people to hate your winning. You need to be able to handle this when it happens, so work on your character.
- The side effect of winning is shining; when you shine, the side effect of shining is reflecting. When you reflect, the people closest to you can see their reflection of their image in your shine. If they don't like how they look in your reflection, they will do one of two things:

So Happy and Grateful

Antonio T.Smith, Jr

Kill your shinning, or leave you so they won' t have to deal with their reflection.

- To deal with family members, friends and loved ones who don' t want to see you winning, love them anyway for who they are and don' t give energy to the hate.

- When you love them for who they are, you give yourself permission for who you are.

1. You don' t owe anyone anything

- You will serve others, but you don' t owe them anything because they have their own life to live and it is their responsibility to create what is worthy of them.

- You can't help people being obligated to them. That is not the same as serving.

- Live your life even if they've decided not to live theirs.

- You don't owe people anything, and neither do they owe you an apology.

- You can help a lot of people as long as you are not in their situation.

So Happy and Grateful

Antonio T.Smith, Jr

1. Don' t live an apology.

- An apology is something you give and it' s done

- If you give an apology with correct motives, and have the appropriate actions to back up this apology, and the other person wants you to hurt as much as they are hurt and not accept your apology, this has nothing to do with you. It has everything to do with that person. That is their bad seed.

So Happy and Grateful

Antonio T.Smith, Jr

1. They have a problem with your life because they have a problem with their own.

   - When you realize the root of their unhappiness is with your winning, you realize it's not your fault or your problem.

Protect Your Dreams

Here is the last thing I will say to you.

We all have dreams we are believing for, things we wish we could turn around, but life teaches us to learn how to live with settling. It is so easy to get discouraged— too easy. Do not let life make you bitter. Do not become defeated. Instead, becoming determined. Human beings are designed to change when we encounter pain. The difficult things are designed to make you better and those things are part of life.

You are not weak, you are well-able. If something in your life has not happened yet, don't get discouraged, get determined. When you become bitter, you become weaker.

So Happy and Grateful

Antonio T.Smith, Jr

Here are a few ways you can begin to protect your dreams.

Be careful with whom you share your dreams.

People can become cruel when they see you doing something in which they do not possess the ability to participate. It is not that they hate you, they just simply hate that they can't be involved in your greatness. You see, every time you shine in your greatness you also show them themselves in your reflection. If someone doesn't like their reflection, they will be confronted with the decision to change themselves or to change you. Most people choose to change you; therefore, they will begin to talk you out of your greatness. All of us experience pain, make sure you don't let others put more pain on you than you deserve.

Watch how you talk to yourself.

You are the only person alive that can stop you from living your dreams. It is easy to settle for mediocrity. Don't! Your insecurities will always whisper to you to bury your dreams. The truth mark of a champion is not winning, but the ability to win beyond the call

So Happy and Grateful

Antonio T.Smith, Jr

of their insecurities. Your insecurities will convince you of what you cannot do. Don't listen to them. This is your time. This is your moment. Shake off the doubt, shake off the negativity. Speak life into your dreams and step into the highest expression of yourself.

Watch how you treat people.

Everything comes back around. If you don't believe in God, believe in Karma. If you don't believe in Karma, then believe in Newton's 3rd Law of Motion. Newton's 3rd law says, "every action has an opposite and equal reaction. " Therefore, if you treat people poorly, people will treat you poorly. What you put out, you will get back. You need to be very careful of how you treat people. All of your blessings, or whatever you wish to call them, will come from people. Life has a way of treating people how they treat people. You may get away with it today, but tomorrow, you will not.

Learn how to say no.

The more you say yes to other people is the more you say no to your own dreams. How can you have enough energy to win in your own life when you spend all your energy winning for someone else. Successful people say no 90% of the time. No is not rude, no is intelligent.

In the words of Will Smith,

"Don' t ever let somebody tell you you can' t do something. Not even me. You got a dream, you gotta protect it. People can' t do somethin' themselves, they wanna tell you you can' t do it. If you want somethin' , go get it. Period. "

Don't Be A Slave To Their Support

Quit waiting for people to approve you and approve yourself. –Joel Osteen

I get to teach people all around the world about change, how to change, and to embrace their change. However, at some point, I have to tell them that they shouldn' t rely on the people who are currently in their lives. Of course, this rarely goes well. However, it is true. Whenever you are transforming your life, you are moving from one level of consciousness to another.

This means, you don't like your life and you want to change it. Okay, that is pretty easy to handle. Now, here is the difficult part: If you want to change your life and you don't like it, the people in your current reality let you be a person that you don't like to be, no longer like to be, or never ever wanted to be. Let's examine this for a second. The people in your life, cousins, parents, spouses, etc., they all allowed you to be the drunk you want to move beyond, the low self-esteemed person you want to move beyond, or the poverty-stricken person you want to

So Happy and Grateful

Antonio T.Smith, Jr

move beyond. In short, they let you be what you hate and they will not be able to support you as the new person you love.

Of course, some of these people mean well, but some of them did not. Some of these people like you where you were because they compared themselves to you and as long as you were lesser than them, they felt like they were better than you, and to be better than you has become a goal in their lives.

Those who do not fit in this category, these are normally your parents, they simply don't have the

So Happy and Grateful

Antonio T.Smith, Jr

level of consciousness that is able to support the new you, because children will never live the life their parents have told them, they will only live the life their parents' have shown them.

Therefore, you are a living and breathing example of what your parents' have struggled with or what they have conquered, this just depends on what were their dominate thoughts and what were the dominant activities that happened within your home. Either way, your future is no longer dependent upon their support, but the support of yourself and the new circle of people you have attracted in your life. Let's talk about it below.

Here are 6 Reasons Why you no longer have to be a slave to their support:

You Are YOUR Priority

Cynthia Kane, a contributor for Elite Daily, wrote this in an article she wrote, that is probably one of the greatest articles I have seen on this subject:

Growing up, I watched other women take care of everyone else. They put others' needs before their own, and they were

praised for it. "Isn't it
wonderful how selfless so and
so is," I'd often hear. But
these selfless women were doing
so much for others that they
often ignored their own needs,
making them unhappy and
unfulfilled. -Cynthia Kane

Yep, this is you and you need to stop it as soon as possible before you kill your dreams trying to serve other people. The truth is, you will never be successful saying yes to 90% of the people in your life. Think about this for a second, if you are always saying yes to them, at least 90% of the time, you are only saying yes to your own dreams 10% of the time. How on earth can you be 100% successful if you only give yourself 10% of your own energy? Your own love, your own worth. To be honest, to be inside the will of your own destiny, is to be outside the will of people. The only power only priority people have over you is the power you give them.

You Are NOT Coming Back

In her book, Me Before You, Jojo Moyes writes:

So Happy and Grateful

You only get one life. It's actually your duty to live it as fully as possible. -Jojo Moyes

This couldn't be more truth if your deity of choice wrote it their self in your sacred scriptures. Your life is yours and you only get one shot at this and you are not coming back. Therefore, you must, and I mean must live it at 100%. No one owes you anything, but you owe you everything. People cannot make you whole, only you can. You are the greatest person of all time.

So Happy and Grateful

Antonio T.Smith, Jr

When you die, that is it. You won' t get a do-over. If you are religious, you believe in an afterlife, but your sacred texts don' t say you get to come back as your dreams and get a second shot at this— nope. You do not have time to live your best life. So, live your best life now.

The Universe Likes Speed

The universe likes speed.

The Universe likes speed. Don' t delay. Don' t second guess. Don ' t doubt. When the opportunity is there, when the impulse is there, when the intuitive nudge from within is there, act— that's your job. And that's all you have to do. -Dr. Joe Vitale

I cannot stress this enough. Dr. Joe Vitale absolutely nailed this. When it is time for you to move towards your dreams, you will not have time to wait for the opinions of others to get what you want. Most people don't have what the want in life because they have conditioned themselves to wait on the approval of others to move forward.

So Happy and Grateful

Antonio T.Smith, Jr

No, you are your permission to move forward. There is no authority, you are your own authority. What you are and who you are will always be what you decide it to be. And when we decide to let others teach us how to live our own lives, we will always live in unhappiness.

Opportunity will wait for no one, even if they are the nicest people on the planet.

They Love You But Don't Want You To Be Better Than Them

Sometimes, the people around us don't want us to be better than them.

Sometimes this happens because they don't like themselves, sometimes this happens because they don't like you. I will break both down. They don't like themselves.

There is a very funny thing about shining brightly. You see, the more you shine, the more you reflect. Basically, when you keep shining, you also keep reflecting. This can create major problems for the people around you who do not like themselves. Think about it. As you are shining in your gifts, you are also showing them their reflection. Therefore, the more you shine, the more they are reminded of how much they are not.

Which also allows them to see who they actually are, and not the lies they keep pretending to be.

In conclusion, when you change for the better, you are a constant reminder to the people who don't love themselves of how much they actually don't love themselves. It is not you that they hate. They hate them. Secondly, some people just don't like you. That is pretty simple to understand. So allow me to address the side of this coin no one likes to observe. This also applies to some of your family. Some of your family doesn't actually like you. They love you, but they don't like you. This is exactly why you can have siblings, but don't actually hang out with them. Why? Just because you are siblings doesn't make you friends.

As long as your motives are correct and you aren't intentionally making people feel bad about themselves, their reaction to your shine will never be your responsibility or your burden.

Gratitude Is The Only Way To Bring More Into Your Life, Not Their Support

So Happy and Grateful

Antonio T.Smith, Jr

Gratitude is the key to everything, not support. You literally have in your life the level of your gratefulness. With this being said, the most important relationship you will ever have is the relationship with yourself. How you feel about you will determine what you get in this life. It will also determine your level of gratitude.

You don't have to be perfect, you will have many shortcomings, but you do not have to be ungrateful. When you are grateful for you, you do not have to be a slave to other people's approval. If you don't like yourself in a healthy way other people are not going to like you, and they most certainly won't support you. If you have a healthy love for yourself and they still don't like you and don't support you, don't take it personally, just understand that these people are not the people for the next level of your life. You are beautiful and your best support.

To be honest, your friends and your family have their own problems. They don't have the time to come home and work on you for three hours.

Don't force people to support you all the time, and don't become a slave to their support either. Let go of the negative things in your life and just relax and know that what you want is already yours.

They Will Probably Never Support You No Matter How Much You Accomplish

Here is the truth: Some of the people in your life have become scared of your potential and they can only cope with this fear by being careful.

It is not that they don't like you, it is that you scare the hell out of them. They don't know what to do with you, they never have, and they never will. You have always been different.

So Happy and Grateful

Antonio T.Smith, Jr

They can' t handle this new you because they couldn' t even handle the old you. So, now, they are afraid. They are afraid of what you can do, and what hurts them the most is this: they have tried to do what you are currently doing and they have failed. They still remember the sting of this pain and they don' t want you to go through it. Their only recourse for you has become caution.

They want to like your status on social media, but if they do you will get more confidence to move forward, and they are afraid if you do, you will get hurt. They want to tell you, "Good job", but if you do, you may actually believe them and achieve your destiny. They don't want that either because poor people always know what is best for you.

Poor people always think they know what is best for you, wealthy people only want what is best for you. Let me release you once and for all. If you have read this far into this blog, you have made it to this moment because you drew this in your life. If it felt good to you, keep it, if not, let it go. When you follow your own heart, you will

So Happy and Grateful

Antonio T.Smith, Jr

always live in a constant state of joy. You don' t need support when you get to this point, you will attract it. You will live in a different reality and a different life, and you will unstoppable.

I can see your future. It is unbounded. It is glorious. It is yours to achieve. See yourself winning, don' t worry about their support. It will come, but it probably won' t come from them. I wrote this blog because something in your kept saying, " I deserve to be happy" , and the universe told me what to write. It told me to

So Happy and Grateful

Antonio T.Smith, Jr

prepare you for the separation from some people and the glorious attachment to the people who will get you to the next level. Who you are and what you do begins right now.

You can plant better. You can dominate.

Antonio T. Smith, Jr.

Transformational Exercise

Let's Connect

Use the hashtag #SoHappyAndGrateful with your blogs, tweets, testimonies, movies, and more, of how this book has changed your life. I will be picking all the ones that move me significantly and feature you on our top-ranked podcast, Brick by Brick-The Motivational Podcast.

So Happy and Grateful

Antonio T.Smith, Jr

Prologue

THE LAW OF ATTRACTION AND THE BIBLE

Chapter 14

I have included this chapter out of kindness. I love all people and assign great value to all religions. I find us

So Happy and Grateful

Antonio T.Smith, Jr

all to be connected and I desire to be at peace with you all. I also understand that in many circles, you are not allowed. If you happen to be of the Christian faith and have been inspired by this book, but would like some material to back up a few things written within, feel free to use this chapter. Although, I have both my Masters and Bachelors in Christian studies, I won't do much interpreting in this chapter. I just want to share with you all the research I did once I was first introduced to the Law of Attraction. Like many of you, I wanted to make sure I was in line with the Bible. This is about 8 years of research. I have kept a running note in my iPhone each year and simply add to it. I want to offer it to you. Remember, I am not trying to change your faith or your theology, and this section will only apply to about one-third of my readers, but it just may be helpful for you as you head back to your churches.

There is something I want you to remember as you get this information. We are all doing the best we can with what we have. Odds are you are being taught greatly and this isn't provide for you to correct anyone. It is just for *in case you need it purposes*, whatever that will mean for you and your life. I love you all. I pray you find this a blessing to you.

Bible Verses That Prove The Law of Attraction

Matthew 8:19

19 Again I say to you, if two of you agree on earth about anything

they ask, it will be done for them by my Father in heaven.

So Happy and Grateful

Antonio T.Smith, Jr

Matthew 21:22

22 And whatever you ask in prayer, you will receive, if you have faith. "

Mark 11:24

24 Therefore I tell you, whatever you ask in prayer, believe that you have received it, and it will be yours.

John 14:13

13 Whatever you ask in my name, this I will do, that the Father may be glorified in the Son.

So Happy and Grateful

Antonio T.Smith, Jr

John 15:7

7 If you abide in me, and my words abide in you, ask whatever you wish, and it will be done for you.

John 15:16

16 You did not choose me, but I chose you and appointed you that you should go and bear fruit and that your fruit should abide, so that whatever you ask the Father in my name, he may give it to you.

John 16:23

23 In that day you will ask nothing of me. Truly, truly, I say to you,

So Happy and Grateful

Antonio T.Smith, Jr

whatever you ask of the Father in my name, he will give it to you.

James 1:5-6

5 If any of you lacks wisdom, let him ask God, who gives generously to all without reproach, and it will be given him. 6 But let him ask in faith, with no doubting, for the one who doubts is like a wave of the sea that is driven and tossed by the wind.

James 1:17

17 Every good gift and every perfect gift is from above, coming down from the Father of lights, with whom there

is no variation or shadow due to change.

1 John 3:22

22 and whatever we ask we receive from him, because we keep his commandments and do what pleases him.

1 John 5:14-15

14 And this is the confidence that we have toward him, that if we ask anything according to his will he hears us. 15 And if we know that he hears us in whatever we ask, we know that we have the requests that we have asked of him.

"Finally, brethren, whatever is true, whatever is honorable, whatever is right, whatever is pure, whatever is lovely, whatever is of good repute, if there is any excellence and if anything worthy of praise, let your mind dwell on these things. " - Philippians 4:8

" There is no fear in love; but perfect love casteth out fear: because fear hath torment. He that feareth is not made perfect in love. " - I John 4:18

"Faith is the substance of things hoped for, the evidence of things not seen. " - Hebrew 11:1

"As a man thinks, so is he. " - Proverbs 23:7

So Happy and Grateful

Antonio T.Smith, Jr

"I will call to mind the deeds of the Lord; I will remember your wonders of old. " - Psalms 77:11

"We do not look at the things which are seen, but the things which are not seen. For the things which are seen are temporary, but the things which are not seen are eternal. " - 2 Corinthians 4:18

"I came that they may have life, and have it more abundantly. " - John 10:10

" I will bless the Lord who counsels me; he gives me wisdom in the night. He tells me what to do. I am

So Happy and Grateful

Antonio T.Smith, Jr

always thinking of the Lord; and because he is so near, I never need to stumble or fall. " - Psalm 16:7-8

"Faith is the assurance of things hoped for, the conviction of things not seen. " - Hebrews 11:1

" Whatsoever things are true, honest, just, pure, lovely, of good report, if there be any virtue, or any praise, think on these things. " - Philippians 4:8

Matthew 21:22 states " And all things, whatsoever ye shall ask in prayer, believe, you shall receive it" .

So Happy and Grateful

Antonio T.Smith, Jr

"···Trust in the Lord, and He will give you the desires of your heart. Commit everything to the Lord. Trust in Him and He will watch over you··· " (Psalm 37:4-5)

"Everything is possible for him who believes. " - Mark 9:23

"For everyone who asks receives; he who seeks finds; and to him who knocks, the door will be opened. " - Matthew 7:8

"I have come that they might have life and that they may have it more abundantly. " - John 10:10

So Happy and Grateful

Antonio T.Smith, Jr

"Beloved I wish that above all things that thou mayest prosper and be in health…" - 3 John 2

"For as a man thinks in his heart, so is he…" Proverbs 23:7

"Make no mistake: God will not be mocked, for a person will reap only what he sows." - Galatians 6:7

"Moreover, God is able to make every grace abundant for you, so that in all things, always having all you need; you may have abundance for every good work." - Second Corinthians 9:8

"Finally, brethren, whatsoever things are true, whatsoever things are

So Happy and Grateful

Antonio T.Smith, Jr

honest, whatsoever things are just, whatsoever things are pure, whatsoever things are lovely, whatsoever things are of good report; if there be any virtue, and if there be any praise, think on these things. " - Philipians 4:8

" A good man out of the good treasure of his heart bringeth forth that which is good; and an evil man out of the evil treasure of his heart bringeth forth that which is evil: for of the abundance of the heart his mouth speaketh. " - Luke 6:35

So Happy and Grateful

Antonio T.Smith, Jr

"For verily I say unto you, That whosoever shall say unto this mountain, Be thou removed, and be thou cast into the sea; and shall not doubt in his heart, but shall believe that those things which he saith shall come to pass; he shall have whatsoever he saith. " - Mark 11:23

1. All powers are ordained by God and subject to God (Job 1:12; Psalms 147:5; Matthew 28:18; John 19:11; Romans 8:38-39; Romans 13:1; Ephesians 3:1-12;

Colossians 1:13-17; Colossians 2:15; 1 Peter 3:22; Jude 1:25)

2. Human minds have no supernatural power of their own (Deuteronomy 8:14-18; Luke 8:22-25; Ephesians 2:1-7; Ephesians 6:10-13; 2 Peter 1:3)

3. Humans do not have the power over death (Ecclesiastes 8:8; Matthew 9:6; Revelation 20:6)

4. Humans can only get power from God (Psalms 68:35; Proverbs 3:27; Ecclesiastes 5:19; Isaiah 40:27-31; Zechariah 4:6; Mark

6:7; Luke 24:49; John 1:12; Acts 1:7-8)

5. Humans that seek powers from other sources, misuse power, or resist the power of God shall be rebuked or damned by God (Deuteronomy 8:19-20; Ezra 8:22; Micah 2:1-4; Luke 4:3-8; Luke 22:53; Acts 8:10; Romans 13:2; 1 Corinthians 9:12-18; 2 Thessalonians 2:8-10; Revelation 13:4-10)

6. The power of God comes only from God (Mark 12:24-27; Luke 10:19; Acts 6:8; Acts 26:14-18; Romans

1:16-20; 2 Timothy 1:7; 2 Peter 1:3)

These are only a fraction of verses that teach us that only God is the I Am (Exodus 3:4); Alpha and Omega (Revelation 1:8); the Word (John 1:1, 14); Healer (Exodus 15:26); Provider (Genesis 22:14); Forgiver (Psalms 99:8); Master (Genesis 15:2); Everlasting (Genesis 21:33); Shepherd (Psalms 23:1); Maker (Psalms 95:6); and Creator (Isaiah 40:28).

"According to your faith be it done unto you." Matthew 9:29

So Happy and Grateful

Antonio T.Smith, Jr

"His favor is for a lifetime."
Psalm 30:5

Proverbs 23:7 For as he thinketh in his heart, so is he. Romans 12:2 And be not conformed to this world: but be ye transformed by the renewing of your mind, that ye may prove what is that good, and acceptable, and perfect, will of God.

Proverbs 23:7 emphasizes the phenomenal power of our thoughts, while Romans 12:2 instructs us to be transformed by the renewing of our minds. As humans, we tend to believe that our thinking changes as the

So Happy and Grateful

Antonio T.Smith, Jr

circumstances of our lives change, but according to the Bible, that simply isn't so. Our lives transform as a result of changed thinking. This simple step lays the foundation for attaining our dreams and goals.

Faith

A Necessary Ingredient Mark 9:23 "Everything is possible for him who believes." Matthew 17:20 He said to them, "Because of your little faith. For truly, I say to you, if you have faith like a grain of mustard seed, you will say to this mountain, " [1] … " Move from here to there, ' and it will move, and nothing will be impossible for you. " Luke 17:6 If you have faith as small as a mustard seed, you can say to this tree, Be uprooted and planted in the sea, and it will obey you. In these verses, God adds one more requirement to receiving that which we desire' " faith. In Matthew 17:20 we learn that with faith anything is possible. Many Christians mistakenly interpret this as faith in God and add a long list of qualifiers to receiving anything from God, but that' s not what the Bible says. It clearly tells us that our faith (or belief) in the power to accomplish the seemingly impossible is the key to manifesting it in our lives.

Receiving Blessings

Matthew 21:22 And all things, whatsoever ye shall ask in prayer, believing, ye shall receive. Luke 11:9 9 "So I say to you: Ask and it will be given to you; seek and you will find; knock and the door will be opened to you. 10 For everyone who asks receives; he who seeks finds; and to him who knocks, the door will be opened. Matthew

9:29 "According to you faith, be it unto you."

Here, we find that in order to receive, we must ask, but asking alone is not enough. We must believe and have faith that what we ask for will be brought to pass. Many fail to ask assuming God knows their needs and will provide for them. Many ask and do not receive and rationalize that it is because "the answer is no", but that's not why the Bible says we fail to receive. The Bible clearly outlines the conditions for receiving'" renew

So Happy and Grateful

Antonio T.Smith, Jr

our thinking, ask, believe and have faith that it will come to pass.

Luke 17:6 - If you have faith as small as a mustard seed, you can say to this tree, Be uprooted and planted in the sea, and it will obey you.

Matthew 7:7 — Ask and ye shall receive.

Mark 11:23 — For verily I say unto you, that whosoever shall say unto this mountain, be thou removed, and be thou cast into the sea; and shall not doubt in his heart, but shall believe that those things which he saith shall come to pass; he shall have whatsoever he saith.

Plus, the Bible has a Code of Conduct

Although the Law of Attraction and the Bible agree in principle on the power of positive thinking and the importance faith, the Bible (being a religious book) suggests a code of conduct related to what you should attract, whereas The Secret (a secular book) does not.

Matthew 6:19 — Do not store up for yourselves treasures on earth, where moth and rust destroy, and where thieves break in and steal. But store up for yourselves treasures in heaven, where moth and rust do not destroy, and where thieves do not break in and steal. For where your treasure is, there your heart will be also.

Matthew 13:22 — The one who received the seed that fell among the thorns is the man who hears the word, but the worries of this life and the deceitfulness of wealth choke it, making it unfruitful.

So Happy and Grateful

Antonio T.Smith, Jr

I saw this written online from someone named ANDREW FREED

The Law of Attraction is not the same as the Law of Sowing and Reaping.

I' ve heard Christians say that the Law of Attraction is the same as the Law of Sowing and Reaping. Not quite. Sowing and reaping requires a physical action as a seed before you can receive or expect to receive a harvest. The Law of

So Happy and Grateful

Antonio T.Smith, Jr

Attraction is activated purely from the thoughts in your mind and the meditations of your heart. It requires no physical activity, however it can be enhanced by it.

The Law of Attraction is not part of the Gnostic Gospel doctrine.

I'm not sure how this one got started. Anyway the Gnosticism is part of the teaching that Peter warns against in 2 Peter 2:1. The premise of Gnosticism is that salvation is obtained through knowledge not Christ. This false doctrine teaches us revelation liberates us from this material world to be in sync with the spirit. This "enlightenment" is primarily what the New Age religion is all about, but it's not New Age at all. It's the same old lie. You see this promoted in the popular movie The Davinchi Code.

Biblical scriptures that support the Law of Attraction

Proverbs 4:23 it states: " Above all else, guard your heart, for everything you do flows from it. " This scripture provides the most support. Solomon was telling us that literally everything we have or will have comes from our heart. The heart has several Hebrew translations, but the word used here is best described as the souls desire and imagination. This

So Happy and Grateful

Antonio T.Smith, Jr

infers that the thoughts that occupy the majority of our thinking gets manifested in our lives. It doesn't matter whether you intended for it to be that way or not. What you think about the most will show up in your life.

Proverbs 23:7 "As a he thinks in his heart, so is he ·· .. " Although this scripture was referring to the miser's heart continually thinking about what it is costing him, it establishes the

So Happy and Grateful

Antonio T.Smith, Jr

principle that what you think about most often you become. We were designed to gravitate to our most dominant thought. In other words, there is a pull, an attraction, to the things that occupy our mental real estate.

Mathew 12:35 Jesus states: "A good man out of the good treasure of his heart brings forth good things, and an evil man out of the evil treasure brings forth evil things."

Jesus was scolding the

Pharisees in reference to their words. He basically said they will speak from the abundance of the heart.   Then He states a man's heart's will bring forth either good or bad, depending on what's in it.   The Greek word for heart used here is psuche' which is also used for the soul.   We also get the English word psyche from this word.   Again it refers to our mind and the dominant thoughts harbored in them.

So Happy and Grateful

Antonio T.Smith, Jr

Genesis 15:1-6, God uses the visualization principle and then in Genesis 17:5 the verbalization principle to bring Abraham to the point where He and Sarah could believe they could have a child in their old age. God told Abram to look at the stars and that's how many descendants he will have (15:1-6) Then God changed Abrams name from Abram, which means fatherless; to Abraham which means father of many. From that moment on every time he saw the stars or he heard his name, all he could think about were his descendants. Nine months later at the ripe old age of 100, he had Isaac.

The Law of Attraction is a powerful tool for faith and success in life. I will share more in future post

The Bible is full of references to the words we speak and the power of the tongue to manifest e. g. "The tongue

So Happy and Grateful

Antonio T.Smith, Jr

has the power of life and death"
(Proverbs 18:21).

Ladies and gentlemen, as children of God, we can SPEAK our reality! All we need to do is to speak a word over ourselves, encourage ourselves in the Lord as David did (1Samuel 1:30).

Luke 17:21 Neither shall they say, Lo here! or, lo there! for, behold, the kingdom of God is within you.

Proverbs 23: 7 For as he thinketh in his heart, so is he.

While pondering the principle of Gratitude and how it can affect every aspect of our lives, I happened upon

the following scripture in Phillipians
4:6

The greek words starting this off
are "meden merimnate" meaning Be not
anxious, as it is also used in Matt
6:25. The next combination however
is even more instructive, "in every
thing, by prayer and supplication,
with thanksgiving," so it is saying
even though we are to not worry about
our needs being met, for they certainly
will be, we are to pray and even
supplicate, which is a bit stronger
word, implying an awareness of lack or

need, with an attitude of thanksgiving.

Psalm 46:10 is a verse in the OT of the Bible

Philip. 4: 6-8

In 1st Thessalonians 5:17-18 it says in the King James version,

17 Pray without ceasing.

18 In every thing give thanks: for this is the will of God in Christ Jesus concerning you.

Jesus in the New Testament often reminded people that it was not by his own power, or that alone that they were healed, but by their faith were they

So Happy and Grateful

Antonio T.Smith, Jr

healed, as in the following from Luke 8: 43-48

Often he said things that were hard to understand regarding faith, such as later in Luke when the Apostles asked for their faith to be increased: Luke 17: 5-6

And the LORD answered me, and said, Write the vision, and make it plain upon tables, that he may run that readeth it. Habakkuk 2:2

Delight thyself also in the LORD; and he shall give thee the desires of thine heart. Psalm 37:4

So Happy and Grateful

Antonio T.Smith, Jr

Everything is possible for him who believes.

Mark 9:23

So do not fear, for I am with you; do not be dismayed, for I am your God. I will strengthen you and help you; I will uphold you with my righteous right hand.

Isaiah 41:10

Don't you know that you yourselves are God's temple and that God's Spirit lives in you?

1 Corinthians 3:

So Happy and Grateful

Antonio T.Smith, Jr

Remember the Lord your God, for it is He who gives you the power to get wealth.

Deuteronomy 8:18

Ask, and it shall be given you; seek; and you shall find; knock and it shall be opened unto you. For every one that asketh receiveth; and he that seeketh findeth; and to him that knocketh it shall be opened.

Matthew 7:7-8

I know the plans I have for you, declares the Lord, plans to prosper you and not to harm you, plans to give you hope and a future.

So Happy and Grateful

Antonio T.Smith, Jr

Jeremiah 29:11

Be strong and courageous. Do not be afraid or terrified because of them, for the LORD your God goes with you; he will never leave you nor forsake you. "

Deuteronomy 31:6

Trust in the Lord with all your heart; and don't lean on your own understanding. In all things acknowledge him, and he shall direct your way.

Proverbs 3:5, 6

There is no fear in love; but perfect love casteth out fear..

1 John 4:18

So Happy and Grateful

Antonio T.Smith, Jr

Come unto me, ye who are weary and
overburdened, and I will give you rest.

‐ Matthew 11:28

The LORD is my light and my salvation‐
whom shall I fear? The LORD is the
stronghold of my life‐ of whom shall I
be afraid?

Psalm 27:1

It is God who arms me with strength
and makes my way perfect.

Psalm 18:32‐36

The earth is full of the goodness
of the Lord.

So Happy and Grateful

Antonio T.Smith, Jr

— Psalms 33:5

Your Father knoweth what things you have need of before you ask Him.

— Matthew 6:8

I will never fail you or forsake you.

— Hebrews 13:5

The Lord will guide you always, he will satisfy your needs in a sun-scorched land. You will be like a spring whose waters never fail.

— Isaiah 58:11

So Happy and Grateful

Antonio T.Smith, Jr

Matthew 7:7- Ask, Seek, Knock

The Gospel of John (14:13) And whatever you shall ask in my name, that will I do, that the Father may be glorified in the Son. ' We must have faith to understand that God will provide for us even if the answers appears to be no.

Jeramiah 29:11 assures us that 'For I know the plans I have for you, " declares the Lord, "plans to prosper you and not to harm you, plans to give you hope and a future.

So Happy and Grateful

Antonio T.Smith, Jr

Proverbs 29:18 (KJV) says 'Where there is no vision, the people perish'

and the book of James (1:6) adds 'But let him ask in faith, nothing wavering. For he that wavers is like a wave of the sea driven with the wind and tossed.'

Combine with Matthew 7:7 and Mark 11:24 'Therefore I say to you, What things soever you desire, when you pray, believe that you receive them, and you shall have them.'

Here are some Bible verses that allude to like attracting like: James

1:13-15, Isaiah 55:8, Matthew 6:33, Matthew 7:7.

I Found This Somewhere. It's Been Years So I Don't Know

What's the truth about the Law of Attraction?

The Law of Attraction truly is a vast topic because of the worldview and the theology, yes the theology, contained within it. I'm going to set the record straight on 12 main points of truth. We'll pick up on some of these in future programs on this New Age series.

So Happy and Grateful

Antonio T.Smith, Jr

1) The Law of Attraction feeds on our desire to be gods or to be as God. It tells us that we alone are the Architects of our lives, the master of our own ships, creators of our own reality, leaving no place for God to be sovereign in our lives. It breeds human self-sufficiency with no need for the true living God. It relies on human wisdom versus divine wisdom. The second lie told on earth was recorded in the Book of Genesis when the serpent, the most cunning of all beasts of the field, told Eve: "you shall be as gods".

So Happy and Grateful

Antonio T.Smith, Jr

2) The Law of Attraction worships the universe – an impersonal energy – as the source of all things. The fundamental theological error here is that the universe is a creation, not a creator. The universe was itself created – it cannot create anything. God alone is the Creator and the universe is His creation. Genesis 1 and 2 describe how God created the universe. When you worship the universe you are engaging in pantheism, worshipping nature gods or energies instead of the one true God.

3) All is not one. The New Thought teaches that everything is a vibrational continuum, that all things are interconnected and ultimately are one, a common belief in pagan religions. This theory by the way is used to explain that thoughts become things, we'll come back to that shortly. The theology of oneness negates the great conflict between good and evil. It gets rid of God and Satan. It also dispenses with sin. Since there is no evil there is no need for law hence there is no sin. Therefore there is no need for Jesus our savior or a plan of salvation.

So Happy and Grateful

Antonio T.Smith, Jr

Jesus is replaced by " Christ consciousness " , a form of right thinking that ' s claimed to bring physical, emotional and spiritual healing.

4) Thanking another power for your blessings dishonors God. When you receive good things in your life and express thanksgiving to a power other than God, you are stealing His glory. God is Jehovah Gyra, the great provider, every good thing comes from Him. Proverbs 10:22 says: "The blessing of the Lord makes one rich,

and He adds no sorrow with it. " Only He can create something out of nothing.

5) Who is the source of your blessings? If you've been using the Law of Attraction and manifesting all kinds of worldly gains, you just might be receiving your blessings from another source. Let's read what Satan said when he tempted Jesus in the desert, this is described in Luke chapter 4: "Then the devil, taking Him up on a high mountain, showed Him all the kingdoms of the world in a moment of time. And the devil said to Him, "All this authority I will give You,

and their glory; for this has been delivered to me, and I give it to whomever I wish. Therefore, if You will worship before me, all will be Yours. " And Jesus answered and said to him, "Get behind Me, Satan. For it is written, ' You shall worship the Lord your God, and Him only you shall serve. ' " If your blessings are coming from a source other than God, you are slave to another master. Romans 6:16 tells us: "Do you not know that to whom you present yourselves slaves to obey, you are that one' s slaves whom you obey, whether of sin leading to death, or of obedience leading to righteousness?" You want to make sure you're serving the right master. Serving Satan always brings sorrow in the end, there's a very high price to pay.

6) The Law of Attraction has no ethics. It promises to give you anything you want, regardless of moral code or consequences. The Bible on the other hand counsels us "Seek ye first the Kingdom of Heaven, and everything else shall be added unto you". In Matthew 6 we read: "Do not lay up for yourselves treasures on earth, where

So Happy and Grateful

Antonio T.Smith, Jr

moth and rust destroy and where thieves break in and steal; but lay up for yourselves treasures in heaven, where neither moth nor rust destroys and where thieves do not break in and steal. For where your treasure is, there your heart will be also. " Or as Jesus put it: "For what profit is it to a man if he gains the whole world, and loses his own soul? Or what will a man give in exchange for his soul?" (Matthew 16:26)

7) Magnetic attraction is not biblical. The Law of Attraction states that we attract things to ourselves

like a magnet, drawing to ourselves things which are in vibrational harmony with our vibration. I found no biblical evidence that like attracts like in this fashion. We do find two bible verses about how the company we keep is or should be in harmony with who we are.

Amos 3:3 - "Can two walk together, except they be agreed?"

2 Corinthians 6:14 - "Be ye not unequally yoked together with unbelievers: for what fellowship hath righteousness with unrighteousness?

So Happy and Grateful

Antonio T.Smith, Jr

and what communion hath light with darkness?

Now, there's a verse that's often cited as biblical proof that like attracts like, and I want to set the record straight on it. Mark 4:25 reads: "For he that hath, to him shall be given: and he that hath not, from him shall be taken even that which he hath." The truth of the matter requires a rather long demonstration of how this text is completely taken out of context. Clearly this verse is important, because it's repeated in three out of the four gospels, in Mark

4 that we just read, in Matthew 13 and in Luke 19. Let's go to Matthew 13. Jesus is teaching the multitude and He always taught them in parables. That day He was expounding the parable of the sower who sowed seeds, some which were blown away by the wind, others were uprooted because they fell among the rocks, and others fell on fertile ground and yielded fruit. Those seeds in the parable represent the Word of God.

In Luke 19 it's a different parable, it's about the master who leaves and entrusts talents to his three servants.

But the teaching point is exactly the same. It has nothing to do with some mystical Law of Attraction where we attract things to ourselves like a magnet. Rather it's simply stating that he who receives little of the Word of God, even that which he received shall be taken away from him because the little he has won't stick, it'll be blown away by the first wind of doctrine or persecution. And he who has received a lot of the Word of God, even more shall be added unto him because his heart is fertile ground and the fruit multiplies. In the other parable

So Happy and Grateful

Antonio T.Smith, Jr

in the gospel of Luke, he who receives talents from God and doesn't t use them or invest them shall have those talents taken away from him, and he who does invest what God has given him, to him it shall be multiplied.

8) Both God and Satan are after our minds. The mind is the real battleground. In the Bible the mind is often referred to as the heart, as we can see from this verse in Proverbs 23:12: " Apply your heart unto instruction, and your ears to the words of knowledge" or in Matthew 9:4 where Jesus speaks to the scribes: " But

Jesus, knowing their thoughts, said, "Why do you think evil in your hearts?" The heart or the mind is the seat of our words and actions, therefore we're instructed to keep or guard our heart. We read in Proverbs 4: "He also taught me, and said to me: Let your heart retain my words; Keep my commands, and live. Get wisdom! Get understanding! Do not forget, nor turn away from the words of my mouth. My son, give attention to my words; Incline your ear to my sayings. Keep them in the midst of your heart; For they are life to those who find them,

So Happy and Grateful

Antonio T.Smith, Jr

and health to all their flesh. Keep your heart with all diligence, for out of it spring the issues of life. "

Throughout the Old Testament God commanded the Israelites to keep His word in their minds. We read in Deuteronomy 11:18: " Therefore you shall lay up these words of mine in your heart and in your soul, and bind them as a sign on your hand, and they shall be as frontlets between your eyes. " Later in Jeremiah the Lord establishes a new covenant with Israel, where He puts His law in their hearts. We are to keep our hearts to protect God's Word and His Law that are inside. Obedience, right speech and right action will be the fruit of that Word. Jesus said "Out of the abundance of the heart the mouth speaks". But nowhere does scripture say that we attract or create our reality with our thoughts as through some mysterious alchemy where thoughts become things in the way that the New Age teaches. This is Satan's ploy to keep us focused on the things of this world.

9) The attraction process is a counterfeit faith. In the movie "The

Secret" the Law of Attraction process is described as " Ask, Believe, Receive", and the universe acts like a magic genie to give you what you want. This is a direct reference to a very key biblical concept we need to examine now, and that is faith. Let's examine some key bible verses about faith, starting with Hebrews 11 verses 1 and 2 which define faith: " Now faith is the substance of things hoped for, the evidence of things not seen. For by it the elders obtained a good testimony. By faith we understand that the worlds were framed by the word of God, so that the things which are seen were not made of things which are visible. " God spoke the universe into existence, the universe is His creation. We didn' t see God create the universe; even Adam and Eve didn' t see Him. But we believe it by faith.

What else does the Bible say about faith?

Hebrews 11:16 - " But without faith it is impossible to please Him: for he that cometh to God must believe that He is, and that He is a rewarder of them that diligently seek him. "

So Happy and Grateful

Antonio T.Smith, Jr

Mark 11:24 - "Therefore I say unto you, What things soever ye desire, when ye pray, believe that ye receive them, and ye shall have them. "

1 Corinthians 2:5 - "That your faith should not stand in the wisdom of men, but in the power of God. "

So Happy and Grateful

Antonio T.Smith, Jr

Romans 10:17 - "Faith comes by hearing, and hearing by the Word of God"

In Matthew 9 we find the story of two blind men healed:

"When Jesus departed from there, two blind men followed Him, crying out and saying, "Son of David, have mercy on us! And when He had come into the house, the blind men came to Him. And Jesus said to them, "Do you believe that I am able to do this? They said to Him, "Yes, Lord. " Then He touched their eyes, saying, " According to your faith let it be to you. " And their eyes were opened. "

What we can conclude from this story and from the other verses we just read is that biblical faith, which is the only true faith, is always in reference to God. There is no faith that can operate outside of the power of God. Faith is a belief in God, that He is able, and that if it' s according to His will He shall give us what we' re asking for. Any faith in any other power than the God of Israel, the God of the bible, is counterfeit, it' s not the true faith. Any supernatural means of obtaining something other than through prayer to God is a counterfeit process.

10) Faith must be aligned with God's will. There is ample biblical evidence that faith definitely works. At almost every miracle Jesus did He said "Your faith has healed you". The only limit to what faith and prayer can accomplish is set by the boundaries of God's will. God has a plan, purpose and vision for each one of us. We are happiest when we are fulfilling that plan and purpose, first because He only wants good things for us, and second

because He knows us better than we know ourselves. When we move away from His plan for us we are being less than we can be, because He always holds the highest vision of us. Let's quickly review some bible verses about the importance of staying within God's will and being obedient to His law so that He will bless us and hear our prayers:

Isaiah 1:19 - "If you are willing and obedient, you shall eat the good of the land"

1 John 5:14-15 - "This is the confidence which we have before Him,

that, if we ask anything according to His will, He hears us. And if we know that He hears us in whatever we ask, we know that we have the requests which we have asked from Him. "

John 9:31 - "We know that God does not hear sinners; but if anyone is God-fearing and does His will, He hears him.

Psalms 66:18 - " If I regard wickedness in my heart, The Lord will not hear"

Isaiah 1:15 - "So when you spread out your hands in prayer, I will hide My eyes from you; Yes, even though you multiply prayers, I will not listen. Your hands are covered with blood. "

Isaiah 59:1-2 - " Behold, the LORD'S hand is not so short That it cannot save; Nor is His ear so dull That it cannot hear. But your iniquities have made a separation between you and your God, And your sins have hidden His face from you so that He does not hear. "

1 Peter 3:12 - "For the eyes of the Lord are toward the righteous, and His ears attend to their prayer, but the face of the Lord is against those who do evil. "

So Happy and Grateful

Antonio T.Smith, Jr

11) There are higher laws than the Law of Attraction. New Age thinkers like to talk about the laws of the universe. More important than the so-called laws of the universe, which are completely fictitious, are the laws of God's government, which apply in heaven, on earth and in the entire universe. God's government is based on the Ten Commandments, which are contained in the heavenly sanctuary and by that standard we shall be judged on the Day of Judgment. The Law of Sin and Death is more important than the Law of Attraction. Sin entered

So Happy and Grateful

Antonio T.Smith, Jr

the universe through Adam and Eve. The Law of Sin and Death says that sin is the transgression of the law and the wages of sin is death. The Law of Justification by Faith says that only by accepting Jesus Christ can our sins be forgiven so that we can escape the penalty of death, since Jesus already died in our place. It's critically important that you understand the laws of God's government and that you live in accordance with them. This is the only way to live eternally. Those who do not comply with these laws shall simply die the first death and receive their reward - the second death or eternal death - after they come in judgment before God.

Satan' s strategy is to keep you bound in trivia so that your mind can' t grasp the enormity of what' s at stake. What difference does it make whether you can attract a 100-dollar bill or a red sports car into your life if you will cease to exist for all eternity?

12) We become what we focus on. We need to focus on Jesus. Everything else is secondary. When we are saved, God gives us a changed heart. God puts His law in our heart and helps us to keep

it. Our job is to keep our focus on Jesus, so that we become like Him and develop a holy character fit for heaven. By beholding we become changed. Philippians 4:8 says: " Finally, brethren, whatever things are true, whatever things are noble, whatever things are just, whatever things are pure, whatever things are lovely, whatever things are of good report, if there is any virtue and if there is anything praiseworthy — meditate on these things. " Then in 2 Corinthians 3:18 - "But we all, with open face beholding as in a glass the glory of the Lord, are changed into the same image from glory to glory, even as by the Spirit of the Lord. " And Hebrews 12:1 - 2 - " Therefore we also, since we are surrounded by so great a cloud of witnesses, let us lay aside every weight, and the sin which so easily ensnares us, and let us run with endurance the race that is set before us, looking unto Jesus, the author and finisher of our faith. "

Have fun and do your own research here. I didn' t interpret much because that will be your job. Love you.

So Happy and Grateful

Antonio T.Smith, Jr

Best,

Antonio T Smith Jr.

So Happy and Grateful

Antonio T.Smith, Jr

About The Author

So Happy and Grateful

Antonio T.Smith, Jr

Antonio T. Smith Jr., born in Galveston,
TX, is a graduate from Houston Baptist
University with a Master of Arts in

So Happy and Grateful

Antonio T.Smith, Jr

Theological Studies and a Bachelors of Arts in Christianity. Antonio is the President and CEO of the ATS Jr. Companies, the Director of Business and Operations with Les Brown Unlimited, business advisor to Les Brown, a speaker, trainer, and coach and a 3 time best-selling author. Antonio is a world leading business expert who travels the world teaching others how to climb out of their trash cans and into their empires and how to make their businesses become profitable. Recently, Antonio has been honored as one of the Top 101 Top Global

So Happy and Grateful

Antonio T.Smith, Jr

Training and Development Minds by the World HRD Congress. His ATS Business University program is helping entrepreneurs become masters in business, sales and marketing and is making those entrepreneurs millionaires. Antonio lives, breathes, and teaches how to dominate.

So Happy and Grateful

Antonio T.Smith, Jr

Connect With Me

Join our online community to stay inspired, network, and to find other *HAPPY PEOPLE.* Visit https://www.facebook.com/groups/peoplewhoplant better/

This book comes with tons of resources for you to stay happy, get happy, and share happiness. Visit

So Happy and Grateful

Antonio T.Smith, Jr

http://sohappyseries.com to access all the resources you need to be happy.

Follow Me Online:

Instagram: http://instagram.com/theatsjr

Facebook: http://facebook.com/theatsjr

Snapchat: https://www.snapchat.com/add/theatsjr

Twitter: http://twitter.com/theatsjr

Be Somebody: http://bit.ly/ATSJRbesomebody

So Happy and Grateful

Antonio T.Smith, Jr

Medium:

http://medium.com/@theatsjr

Subscribe on one of these platforms.

Podcast Apple |
http://apple.co/2pAUvvZ

Podcast
Stitcher|http://bit.ly/2pB29GJ

Podcast
Podomatic |http://bit.ly/2pBdwyr

Sound Cloud Podcast|
https://soundcloud.com/brickbybrickp
od

Podcast Overcast
http://bit.ly/2wRYDNb

So Happy and Grateful

Antonio T.Smith, Jr

Podcast   Tune
In|http://bit.ly/2uDiF9t

Podcast
Spreaker|https://www.spreaker.com/us
er/antoniotsmithjr

YouTube | http://bit.ly/SubPlzATS

Speaker   Hub |
https://speakerhub.com/speaker/anton
io-t-smith-jr

Les   Brown   Unlimited |
http://www.lesbrownunlimited.com

Made in the USA
Middletown, DE
08 March 2019